Visionary Chicago Architecture

Fourteen Inspired Concepts for the Third Millennia

For Mayor Richard M. Daley

Edited by
Stanley Tigerman and
William Martin

**Published by
Chicago Central Area
Committee**

Edited by
Stanley Tigerman
William Martin

ISBN 0-9762280-0-9

Preface

For a half century the Chicago Central Area Committee has been a guiding force in shaping the future of Chicago's Downtown. As President of this organization, I feel a strong responsibility to continue our mission of creating visionary concepts for our great City. The works in this book represent our continued commitment to our civic responsibility, and are a testament to the strong partnership between Chicago's public and private sectors.

The work of the fourteen architects and authors, represented on the following pages, was a labor of love for the city they love. They have graciously contributed their time and, more importantly, their creative talents to help define a vision for Chicago. That these individuals were willing to commit to a project of this magnitude confirms that the "I Will" spirit is alive and well in Chicago. Just as that spirit brought Chicago back from the ashes of the "Great Fire" to become the magnificent city it is today, I am convinced that this resolve will guide us to a future that will be envied and emulated.

I am proud to dedicate this book to Mayor Richard M. Daley, whose tenacity and love of this city has turned visions into reality. Navy Pier, the Museum Campus and Millennium Park, to name a few, once were just ideas. Today, these grand public amenities are enjoyed by Chicagoans and all who visit. Hopefully, the visions presented on the following pages will provide an inspiration for the future of this great city.

Carrie J. Hightman
Chicago Central Area Committee
President

3

Forward

Chicago architecture transcends generations and makes a memorable impression on our lives. To grow up here and experience life set in an urban backyard masterfully appointed by the historic architecture of Louis H. Sullivan, Mies van der Rohe and Daniel Burnham, to name only a few of the great architects who have defined our skyline, is to be forever influenced by the power of environment and how structure and space define and build the way we work, play and live as people and communities in this great, metropolitan city.

Daniel Burnham said long ago to make no little plans, to aim high in hope and work and to remember that one day our grandchildren will do things that will stagger us. His message still resonates today. He is the father of a vision for the city that we have never lost sight of, and the architects you will read about within these pages are undoubtedly the descendants of a dream on the brink of realization.They are the grandchildren of Burnham who will stagger us with plans for Chicago as alive and diverse and significant as the people and families who live here.

As the Executive Director of the Chicago Central Area Committee, I first discovered my love of city planning as a young boy. Born and raised in downtown Chicago, I would play in the sandbox at Grant Park, and I was always more interested in constructing the environment around which things were built than the actual buildings themselves. Back then, my father managed the Chicago Theater, and my mother worked a block down the street on Michigan Avenue. This area has always been part of my life, and I'm pleased to call this neighborhood my home. There is a tremendous value to cherishing a home and community and to give back so that younger generations may continue to flourish and stagger us all the more. Through hard work, good luck and the guidance of several people who've served as invaluable mentors in my career, I am proud to be part of an effort conceived long ago that is now being brought to fruition through the joined accomplishments of today's masters. We simultaneously give nod and homage to the past and present as history is recognized through works of these architects, whose result will reshape our future and ultimately improve the way we live.

Tom Cokins
Chicago Central Area Committee
Executive Director

Overview

Perhaps the most enduring memento of the Columbian Exposition – the larger-than-life fruit of extraordinary toil that put Chicago on the global map – is the oft quoted admonition of the fair's Director of Works, Daniel Burnham: "Make no little plans; they have no magic to stir men's blood." Visionary and prophetic, his plans and words did indeed stir men's blood. Their impact is abundantly evident in Chicago's architectural heritage and contemporary cityscape, from parks, boulevards and bridges to housing, schools and transportation.

Chicago has always been a city to think big. Movers and shakers, private and civic, historically have joined forces to forge a city that long ago resolved to be second to none. Maybe the broad prairie and limitless sky have inspired our city's urge to harness the energy of nature and open spaces.

But without a doubt, opportunity, motivation, ingenuity and vision have contributed to expansion from a modest lakefront settlement, reconstruction from a devastated bed of ashes, reversal of the river's flow, rerouting a lakefront highway, the first skyscraper, and construction of the world's tallest building, to name just a few notable feats.

Our predecessors set the precedent. Collectively and as individuals we continue to breathe life into the spirit of Burnham's simple yet eloquent challenge. Over more than a century, the proverbial blood of mayors, business leaders, industrial titans, prominent citizens and ordinary working folks has been stirred to deeds that aim to make Chicago a better place tomorrow than what it was yesterday or what it is today.

Jim DeStefano
Chicago Central Area Committee
Board of Directors

contents

07 Stanley Tigerman

12 Robert Bruegmann

17 Jeanne Gang

27 Ron Krueck

37 Brad Lynch

47 Joe Valerio

57 Doug Garofalo

67 John Ronan

77 David Woodhouse

103 Adrian Smith

113 Helmut Jahn

123 Dirk Lohan

133 Ralph Johnson

143 Carol Ross Barney

153 Larry Booth

163 Tom Beeby

173 Lee Bey

key

a) Ohio/Ontario Gateway

b) Northerly Island

c) Chinatown Gateway

d) The Chicago River

e) The Loop "El"

f) The Old Post Office

g) South Loop
   Educational District

GOOSE
ISLAND

NEAR
NORTH

THE
MAGNIFICENT
MILE

STREETERVILLE

Navy Pier

a RIVER
NORTH

Ohio

NEAR
WEST
SIDE

LaSalle

Wacker

Lake

d

THE
LOOP

e

State

LAKE MICHIGAN

Halsted

NEAR
WEST
SIDE

f

Congress

g

PRINTERS
ROW

SOUTH
LOOP

Northerly
Island

b

NEAR
SOUTH
SIDE

c

CHINATOWN

The Value of Visionary Architecture
Seven Projects; Fourteen Architects
Stanley Tigerman

In the autumn of 2003, Chicago Central Area Committee's Urban Planner Bill Martin and I reminisced over lunch about Chicago's powerful physicality, and the circumstances that have periodically skewed the city's trajectory by exploring visionary artistic vis-à-vis architectural enterprise. We wondered if ours was one of those eras when visions of the future imagined by forward-looking Chicago architects working in different métier, might stir our collective civic pride. Assuming that we could organize such an event, we thought that our efforts might possibly lead to the initiation of a ground swell of activities emanating from Chicago's cultural community edifying the extraordinary circumstances in which we Chicagoans find ourselves in the early years of this new millennium.[1]

At several seminal moments throughout our city's history, visionary architecture gave flesh to Chicagoan's dreams about their future. Item: Louis Sullivan's pragmatic/poetic response to the conflagration of 1871 - architectural historians later elevated his and his colleague's otherwise constructionally pragmatic efforts to the status of art by referring to their work as constituting a first "Chicago School of Architecture." Item: Daniel Burnham's (together with his largely East Coast colleague's) derivative regurgitations informing the 1893 Columbian Exposition posited as a "White City" and later Burnham's 1909 Plan of Chicago (with Jules Guerin's highly charged renderings), had a visionary, albeit "retro" quality about them. Item: The optimism embedded within Frank Lloyd Wright's domestic work, emanating from his Oak Park-based studio's production inspired architectural inter-pretations about America's Midwestern prairie fairly shouting "Go west, young man," which caused our spirits to soar. Item: Chicago's Wacker Manual was produced during the Great Depression as a manifestation of the "City Beautiful Movement" thus helping to reverse perceptions about the otherwise difficult times. Item: Mies van der Rohe's "second coming" of yet another "Chicago School of Architecture" - this one situated in reductivist structural expression - gave Chicago's City Fathers hope for a future[2] embedded within the optimism, as well as the existential fact (to say nothing of the commercial usefulness) - of the amalgam of the art and science of architecture.

Thus it is that at the turn of the Twenty-first Century, we find ourselves once again yearning for inspiration to inform our collective future here in our urban oasis situated at the seam between our Sweetwater sea and it's endless Midwestern prairie.

For almost five decades, Chicago's Central Area Committee (CCAC)[3] has periodically published several "Central Area Plans" consulting with members of Chicago's architectural community who responded by serially suggesting functionally useful iterations of our city's Central Business District. Often, these plans were so swept along by the hoped-for potential of being realized (after all, they were initiated by leaders of Chicago's business community who had it within their power to actualize the ideas that they themselves caused to transpire), that whatever visionary dreams they might have otherwise suggested were never entirely fulfilled. Even now, the CCAC persists in envisioning certain sites - 'gateways' - that could celebrate entering into a city understandably in thrall to a mayor determined to making Chicago at once the most lushly beautiful as well as the most ecologically and environmentally responsible bit of urban geography in the United States.

For these reasons (combined with our own innate love of Chicago), Bill Martin and I assembled two teams of seven architects each - one group less established, somewhat younger (thus, by nature more spontaneous),[4] the other group more established, somewhat ripened (and by definition, more sophisticated).[5] We asked each architect to address conceptually each of seven gateway sites[6] in the spirit of the best historical efforts within Chicago's considerable visionary precedents. Each group was to meet periodically within their own collective cross-critiquing each other's concepts. By virtue of each group meeting separately, the designer of a particular site would neither be privy to, nor contaminated by, the designs that his or her counterpart envisioned. Nonetheless, we were aware of the competitive aspect that the basic enterprise inferred. The charge to each architect was to evolve a concept that would be informed largely by visionary ambitions within the context of their individual site(s), while still being arguably buildable in the foreseeable future. The resulting project that each architect envisioned (statements of intentionality, preliminary conceptual sketches and final designs) constitutes the body of this book.

Virtually all of the selected sites were approached in entirely different ways unique to the particular architect, as well as to each individual site.

Example: Jeanne Gang imagined the Ohio/Ontario gateway as an opportunity to stitch the city back together as a belated response to the disruption caused by the Kennedy Expressway with a produce market/migratory bird sanctuary concealing support trucking beneath it. Alternatively, Adrian Smith looked into the future where he envisioned different kinds of transportation - literal as well as virtual - at several horizontal registrations (including the conventional one at grade).

8

Ohio/Ontario Gateway — Jeanne Gang / Adrian Smith

Northerly Island — Ron Krueck / Helmut Jahn

Chinatown Gateway — Brad Lynch / Dirk Lohan

The Chicago River — Joe Valerio / Ralph Johnson

The Loop "El" — Doug Garofalo / Carol Ross Barney

The Old Post Office — John Ronan / Larry Booth

South Loop Educational District — David Woodhouse / Tom Beeby

Example: Ron Krueck dealt with Northerly Island by developing a topologically complex, yet comprehensive recreational zone that he refers to as a "Sensescape." On the other hand, Helmut Jahn situated a North-South pedestrian spine reminiscent of the former Meigs Field runway anchored by an environmentally derived rotating tower spiked into the ground, both components of which act as access points to recreational zones.

Example: A kind of Yin-Yang at the Chinatown gateway finds Brad Lynch designing an extremely long horizontal parking garage acting as a symbol for this traditionally ethnic precinct, while Dirk Lohan erects the same transportation program vertically, as a mammoth robotically controlled parking garage coincident with other transportation elements (on both land and water).

Example: Joe Valerio produces a water museum/turning basin at the juncture of Lake Michigan intersecting with the main branch of the Chicago River at its easternmost point, whereas Ralph Johnson anchors both ends of the main branch of the Chicago River with public park-like amenities, while at the same time linking up with other (earlier) design proposals of his as well.

Example: Doug Garofalo enlivens the elevated train structure defining the "Loop" by situating a series of differentiated functional civic and recreational elements off that corridor. On the other hand, Carol Ross Barney expands upon the linear Loop spine in three dimension by designing above-grade park-like elements that contain various public uses, as well as appropriating underdeveloped sites adjacent to that spine.

Example: John Ronan envisions the Old Post Office as an urban mortuary providing future Chicagoans with an opportunity to have a repository for their remains, replete with river-bound funerary vessels processionally plying the Chicago River on their way to ceremonial functions held within the existing structure. Larry Booth approached the project as a commercial, parking and housing zone, with a recreational precinct and rotating bridge where this gateway literally cleaves through the old post office itself.

Example: David Woodhouse suggests unifying the metropolitan core as a precinct completely distinct from others by positing a lighting - graphics rectilinear gridded structure at a registration far above grade to uniquely define the overall area. Tom Beeby creates a "Pattern Book" defining metropolitan building types that opportunistically respond to the challenges of urban intensification.

To say the least, the lively, often disparate design ideas that constitute the body of what follows is multivalently invigorating.

In order to comment appropriately about the project, Bill and I asked the noted architectural historian Robert Bruegmann to prepare a text that would situate the enterprise historically.

9

Representing the Chicago Central Area Committee, it's 2004/05 President Carrie Hightman honored us with a preface, the CCAC's Executive Director Tom Cokins has written a forward, and architect/CCAC board member Jim DeStefano has weighed in on these fourteen visions in relationship to prior Central Area plans (with which he was familiar since, over time, he worked on several of them). Finally, we asked the journalist/ urban critic Lee Bey to establish a contemporary context in which these projects might best be understood as we collectively move toward Chicago's future.

A preliminary meeting was held with each group of seven architects informing them of our ambitions,[7] and all fourteen of those initially identified enthusiastically agreed to participate[8] without knowing who their counterparts might be. Four subsequent "critiques" occurred (two each per chronological division),[9] at which time the architects from each category critiqued their colleagues' schemes.[10] Each of the four sessions was recorded by a court reporter. These notes were later transcribed, excerpts of which will be found on the concluding (10th) page of each of the architect's sections.

In addition, photos were taken recording each of the working sessions, many of which are included here inside the front and back cover so as to convey a sense of the process, so that the product, might transparently represent the entire affair.[11]

On October 28, 2004, all fourteen participants met in order to turn over their architectural production for purposes of editing, not incidentally seeing the individual proposals of the "other" group for the first time at that final meeting. I believe that I'm accurate in reporting that the entire process was optimistically spirited, with virtually all of the participants determined to produce work at their highest and best capacity.

The work speaks for itself. The extraordinary energy of all the participants represented within these pages is exemplary, to say nothing of the intensity of the (pro bono) effort expended by each participant.[12] As noted earlier, each site is dealt with unique to its own context, suggesting that Chicago architects are not held captive by design preconceptions delimiting individual architectural expression. The resulting freedom of ideation is duly noted here (and, I hasten to add, applauded). Freedom, in this case, should not be misconstrued as "anarchy" - it simply represents an openness to what each architect felt was appropriate for the situation at hand without subscribing to International Style Modernism, neo-Miesianism, Historicism, Post-Modernism, Deconstuctivism, or any other "ism" that might be in vogue.

The tyranny of earlier structural expression that may have influenced successor designers in Chicago to any of our several "heroic" epochs [13] appears to have been replaced by a level of unbridled, optimistically inclined innovation bereft of preconception not seen in Chicago for some time.

Of course, we hope that both the public and the private sectors of Chicago's development community become sufficiently excited by the many unique ideas posited here, and more importantly, that they use their considerable authority to cause these concepts, and others like them, to be implemented. Given the incredible environment that Chicago's leadership (specifically Mayor Richard M. Daley) has caused to transpire, it seems fitting that significant gateways come into being so as to announce one's arrival into our (now) glorious urban environment. Capping those initiatives is the Mayor's determination that Chicago be perceived as the most environmentally responsible city in the nation. It is appropriate that this book is dedicated to his own forward-looking approach to our city's physical environment. Not only has he made Chicago a paradigm for other American cities, but he has also challenged Chicago's architects to contend with the ecological challenges necessary to our survival by designing appropriately (and responsibly).

On some level then, this project is positioned well within the visionary guidelines historically established rising out of the ashes of the 1871 fire, as imagined initially by Louis Sullivan, Martin Roche, William le Barron Jenney and company, later as re-envisioned by Daniel Burnham (and a quarter-century later in the "Wacker Manual"), and finally, as broad-based conceptual revolutions initiated first by Frank Lloyd Wright and later by Mies van der Rohe. The similarity between earlier conceptually driven architects and those (both older and younger) included in this publication, is that neither was particularly constrained by that which defined each of their epochs. While Chicago's architectural visionaries of the past eras mentioned here clearly expanded the architectural palette, their sycophantic descendants (who perhaps followed too closely on the heels of Chicago's great revolutionary figures) didn't always add to the language of those who preceded - and influenced - them. It is no small matter that our own contemporary architects are so open to ideas informed by a watershed era. This bodes well for an architecturally inclusivist future no longer delimited stylistically, but intrinsically fresh, positioned well within a multivalent culture committed to change technologically, ecologically AND humanistically, by responding responsibly to social and environmental issues as the bookends of a new, democratically driven norm.[14]

Our aspirations for this book not only rely on the particularities of what is situated within these pages, but upon a future periodically in need of conceptual vigor when the circumstances warrant it. From time to time, the body politic requires stimulation so as to reinvigorate - and reposition its direction. If there's anything to learn from Chicago's architectural history, it's just that. Chicago's openness to large-scale change has continuously redefined us. That these fourteen architects have stimulated us with their generosity, their spirit, as well as their bold ideas, does not go unnoticed in an era not always characterized by its forthcoming nature.

I want to thank them - all fourteen of them - for responding positively and promptly to our city's needs - as well as to its aspirations. One can only hope that this book will inspire future generations of architects as well as other cultural and artistic enterprises to pick up this baton and to run with it.

(1) The city has never looked so good. The completion of Millennium Park, the 'greening' of the city (boulevards, building roofs, et al), refurbished Park District structures, and many other visible amenities made available for public usage, suggests that a new day is in store for native Chicagoans and visitors alike.

(2) Mies van der Rohe came to Chicago in 1937, i.e., when America was in the throes of the Great Depression - and, not so incidentally when we were about to embark on what came to be known as WWII. Thus, the optimism to which I allude was certainly welcome after nearly two decades of marking time.

(3) The Chicago Central Area Committee is a public charitable trust legally constituted as an IRS approved 501(c)3). Its membership is composed of civic, commercial, cultural and professionals representing virtually all aspects of Chicago's central business district leadership.

(4) The seven generally (but not entirely) younger, somewhat less established architects are: Jeanne Gang, Douglas Garofalo, Ronald Krueck, Bradley Lynch, John Ronan, Joseph Valerio and David Woodhouse.

(5) The seven generally (but not entirely) older, somewhat more established architects are: Carol Ross Barney, Thomas Hall Beeby, Laurence O. Booth, Helmut Jahn, Ralph Johnson, Dirk Lohan and Adrian Smith.

(6) The seven "gateway" projects are: the Ohio/Ontario connector (at Orleans), The Loop "El" (Wells, Van Buren, Wabash and Lake), Northerly Island (most recently home to Meigs Field airport), the near South Chinatown Gateway precinct, the Old Post Office (gateway to/from the West), the Main Branch of the Chicago River (Wolf Point to Lake Shore Drive) and the South Loop Educational District.

(7) The "younger" group first met on November 26, 2003 at the Central Area Committee's offices, and the

"older" group met subsequently on January 7, 2004. Both groups were informed of our intentions, sites were assigned by "lottery" and a general schedule was agreed upon.

(8) The participating architects were not necessarily selected as Chicago's "best-of-breed," but rather as exemplary leaders within the discipline, of which others at the same level of capability within the two chronologies would be arguably equal to the tasks assigned.

(9) The "younger" group's critiques were held on April 7, and July 27, 2004, and the "older" group's critiques were held on April 14, and July 22, 2004.

(10) We asked that only the named architect on each project be present at the critiques, since these designs were to represent the particular individuals selected - not their firms. Of course, we understood that others who were associates and/or employees of those listed above might well produce some of the final documentation, and indeed such assistance is so credited by the selected architects as they saw fit.

(11) We felt that both the audiotaping and the photographic documentation of the process were important as a record of the proceedings. Given Chicago's history of visionary architectural production mentioned earlier, it seemed only fitting that future scholar have access to both process and product.

(12) While we tried to incorporate the entirety of each architect's efforts, there was simply not enough space to include absolutely all of their rather significant production.

(13) An all too-well known Chicago condition (Sullivanesque, Burnhamesque, Wrightian, Miesian, ad infinitum) referring to sycophantic successors, and not to the original innovators themselves.

(14) This new condition of openness is virtually (but not entirely) bereft of nostalgia, and/or a sense of "the picturesque."

The City as Work of Art in a Democratic Society

Robert Bruegmann

According to Stanley Tigerman, there were two major reasons for inaugurating the Chicago Vision project. The first was that he sensed a widespread perception that Chicago architecture had lost its critical edge, that it no longer had architects like Louis Sullivan or Mies van der Rohe who not only changed the face of the city but influenced the practice of architecture around the world. Tigerman wanted to do something to dispel this idea and prove that architectural creativity was alive and well in the Windy City. He also wanted to give the people of Chicago some new ideas about how design could solve some aesthetic and practical problems. His vehicle for both aspirations, worked out with Bill Martin of the Chicago Central Area Committee, was a cross between a design charrette, a short-term studio experience organized by a group of design professionals

to generate ideas about solving a particular urban problem, and an architectural ideas competition. In this process, two teams of invited architects, among them some of the most prominent in the region, would produce designs for specific sites in the city. They would meet at fixed intervals in the design process and share the results with one another. The final schemes would be presented to the city and to the public at large through this book.

Remarkably enough, everything went according to plan. Tigerman, who is often blunt and direct, can also be a generous and galvanizing influence, and this project showed him at his best. The architects he assembled, a group that boasts some of the most oversized egos in the business, actually spent a great deal of time on their assigned projects, came to the meetings and

listened to criticism of their work. They then went back to the drawing board and reworked their schemes. The final projects shown on these pages are interesting not only in their own right but also for what they reveal about current thinking about architectural design, urban planning and the role of the architect in the city.

One of the things that this entire exercise suggests is a dramatic shift in the way the old industrial city functions and is perceived. Although, throughout history, there have been cities whose function seems to have been primarily administrative and ceremonial, the majority of cities have been largely utilitarian. This was particularly true of manufacturing centers in the industrial age – Manchester or Birmingham in Britain, Essen or Düsseldorf in Germany or Pittsburgh or Chicago in the United States. In the case of the ceremonial cities, kings and religious leaders often expended vast sums of money making and remaking parts of the urban fabric to form a fitting backdrop for their regimes. In Rome the popes of the Renaissance and Baroque era spent fabulous sums of money driving new streets through existing urban fabric and out through open fields to provide a setting for immense churches and palaces that would awe pilgrims to the city. The same largesse was visible in Paris where rulers from Louis XIV through Francois Mitterrand spent public money liberally to remake the city, in part to solve practical problems but also to demonstrate the wealth and power of the French state.

Industrial cities, on the other hand, rarely benefited from this kind of munificence. Cities like Chicago were primarily places to make money. Still, once they become affluent enough, citizens of industrial cities almost invariably start to yearn for cultural institutions and grand buildings.

The creation of the Art Institute and the Chicago Public Library, as well as the Burnham Plan of 1909 demonstrated these aspirations at the turn of the Twentieth Century. Although this push toward order and elegance was somewhat submerged during the difficult years at mid-century when the city was reeling under the pressure of job loss and competitions from the suburbs, it has resurfaced in recent years during a pronounced resurgence in the economy of the Chicago region, and along with it, a striking gentrification of the Loop and inner city neighborhoods.

In this process of gentrification, most of the manufacturing operations, warehousing and back-office functions that once filled buildings in the Loop have left for the suburbs. Along with them have gone the working class families that manned these establishments and the poor immigrants that used to occupy the oldest and most decrepit housing nearby.

Chicago's central business district increasingly revolves around high-end business, government, tourism, culture and an affluent residential population. This new population has fueled a major drive to clean up and embellish the center of Chicago. One of the greatest political strengths of Mayor Richard M. Daley has been his interest in design as a way to make day-to-day life more pleasant for affluent new residents and to make Chicago economically more globally competitive.

Architectural design has been an important chip in the high-stakes game of urban global competition. Among the most successful players have been Paris with its "grands projets;" Barcelona with its Olympic buildings and new parks; and London with its new Tate Modern Gallery and structures by architects like Richard Rogers and Norman Foster. Perhaps the most spectacular recent example has been the Spanish industrial city of Bilboa whose Frank Gehry - designed

Guggenheim Museum has virtually overnight introduced the "wow factor" into discussions of urban revitalization.

A common lament among American architects, particularly young American architects, is how conservative American cities are and how little chance they have to make a major mark on the face of the metropolis. They compare their situation with that of their European peers who seem to be able to build important public buildings by winning public competitions. However, it is not always clear that the population of some of these European cities actually appreciates designs made for them by upper-middle-class architects and government bureaucrats who have very different aesthetic sensibilities. Nevertheless, there has been a marked upsurge in the number of competitions for sites in American cities, the competitions for Ground Zero in New York being the most conspicuous examples.

In Chicago, the last few years have witnessed a remarkable outpouring of design ideas sparked by competitions. In the last few months the Chicago Architecture Foundation exhibited the results of a competition for bridges over the Lake Shore Drive and the Graham Foundation a set of schemes for the extension northward of the Chicago lakefront park. The schemes in this book represent a parallel effort to use the skills of architects to analyze the city, discover poorly utilized areas of urban fabric and to create designs that can uncover their potential. Several of these schemes aim to reclaim and polish parts of the very heart of the city. Doug Garofalo and Carol Ross Barney, for example, take as their point of departure the Loop elevated structure. They respect the elevated structure but envision a friendlier, greener experience along the transit corridors. Tom Beeby and David Woodhouse imagine new structures

for a Loop that no longer provides workplaces for manufacturing workers but is now home to tens of thousands of students, and Ralph Johnson and Joe Valerio contemplate ways to increase the amenity value of the Chicago River, which has become increasingly less important as a working river and more important as a recreational and scenic asset.

The schemes in this book aren't merely an attempt to create monuments, though. Like Daniel Burnham in his Plan of Chicago, a great many use design to solve urban problems. Many of these involve transportation. Ralph Johnson and Brad Lynch imagine rerouting transportation lines at once to make the transportation more efficient and to free up land for new, more rational development. Larry Booth suggests an intermodal transportation center on the site of the Old Post Office with a residential village on top of it. Dirk Lohan proposes a great tower in Chinatown not only to give this community a new monumental presence but also to deal with the fact that it sits at the end of a freeway spur. Other kinds of urban problems are addressed as well. Ralph Johnson proposes a high-rise SRO to accommodate homeless people at a site on the Chicago River, and, in one of the most dramatic of all the schemes, John Ronan transforms the Old Post office into an enormous public mausoleum.

These schemes also provide interesting commentary on one of the fundamental issues in architecture today – its relationship with planning. In the early twentieth century many of the most famous planners in the world – figures like Henri Prost or Leon Jaussely in France or Daniel Burnham in the United States – were trained as architects. As the old Beaux-Arts system yielded to the newly emerging European modernism, not just classical architectural design but the traditional land use planning were abandoned in favor of great abstract schemes that had little to do with traditional urbanism. Eliminating the traditional street and block pattern and creating compositions that looked more like abstract sculpture than traditional cities was the order of the day. Both modernist planning and architecture came under fire in the 1970s as being arrogant, inhumane and not sufficiently attuned to environmental conditions. Several of the architects in this project, but particularly Stanley Tigerman, were major figures in the so-called "post-modern" reaction to orthodox modern architecture and planning.

Since then there has been a marked revival of Modernist style architecture as witness the vast majority of the schemes in this book. But there has been much less interest in reviving modernist planning. Most of the schemes here respect at least some of the traditional ordering principles of traditional cities, reproducing the pattern of streets and blocks, sidewalks, parks and other urban elements but re-interpreting them in arresting new ways. Perhaps the most overt attempt to create a new urban order is the scheme by Adrian Smith who has imagined a "city of the future" where the bottlenecks of ground transportation have been solved by personal air travel. His alluring scheme of great towers, because of its resemblance to science fiction projects of the early twentieth century, seems curiously familiar, almost nostalgic.

Perhaps the most striking thing visible in these schemes is a turn from architecture to landscape as a basic ordering device for urban design. During the heyday of the great industrial cities, landscape became an almost negligible factor in many cities except where it seemed to survive in a few parks. In many cases it was hard to imagine that there had ever been a natural landscape under the unrelenting expanse of masonry. Perhaps because of the contemporary city's new, more upscale, functions and perhaps as a reaction to the lower densities and greater attention to landscape visible in the suburbs, today's cities are becoming greener. Although a number of the schemes, notably those by Garofalo, Ross Barney and Gang, involve substantial new landscape elements, it is the projects of Helmut Jahn and Ron Krueck that make most conspicuous the relationship of city to land. In their projects for Northerly Island, an artificial piece of land in the lake, they imagine an urban fabric that is neither traditional park nor traditional city but a bold merger of the two, frankly manmade but nevertheless deeply connected to the natural world.

Above all, the Chicago Vision project provides an interesting example of the process of imagining and designing cities in a democratic society. In the Paris of Louis XIV or Baron Haussmann this issue was not really important. Good design, it was assumed, could be dictated from on high, and it was lavished on places like central Paris. Today, with the changing role of the industrial city, a vast increase in wealth, and gentrification, it is possible to imagine even a place like central Chicago as a work of art. But this possibility raises serious questions. Whose standards of taste should prevail? Do avant-garde architects have the duty or the right to impose their preferences on the public? Who is the client for projects like the ones presented in this book? All of these questions remain to be worked out. In the meantime, projects like these can play an important role in arousing public interest in what the architect can offer the city and in demonstrating new possibilities in urban design.

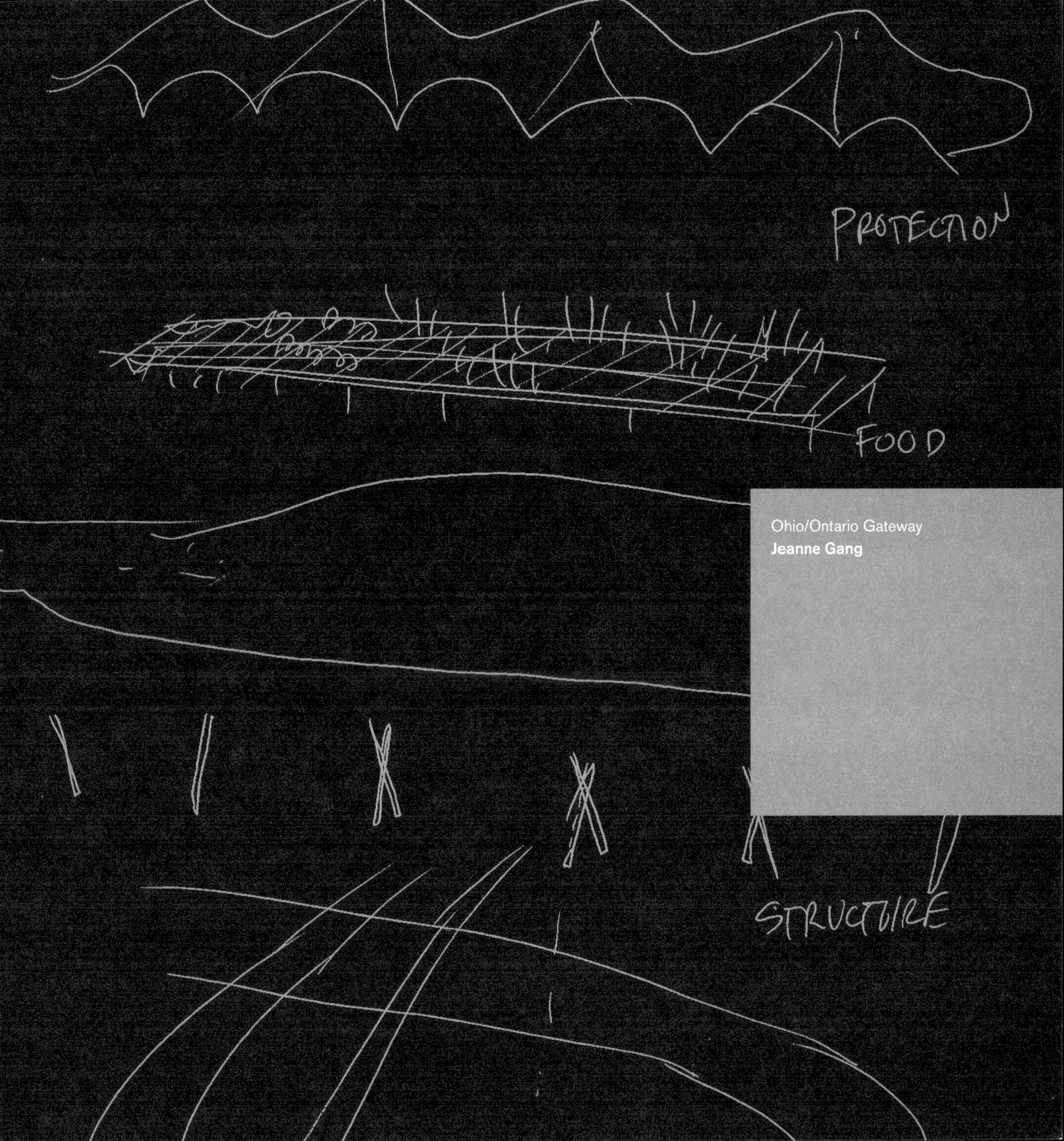

PROTECTION

FOOD

Ohio/Ontario Gateway
Jeanne Gang

STRUCTURE

Ohio Feeder Gateway

Chicago is a great place to live; many come here to dwell in this bountiful urban habitat for people. Habitats are places that provide food, shelter and mobility. Our buildings (shelters) and highways (mobility corridors) are highly visible features while food production is typically hidden from view.

Ohio Feeder Gateway is my proposal to magnify and expose the important aspect of food production as a necessity for urban living. The project combines a series of highly productive hothouses, gardens and landscaped areas exploiting the underutilized open space of highway interchanges. It offers a useful and productive gateway architecture that reinvigorates Chicago as an urban habitat.

The loss of adjacent farmland to development bordering the City means that food must be transported further and further to reach our dense population in Chicago. It takes 12.5 acres of land to feed one person for a year with traditional farming. Hothouse production feeds 36 times more people on the same amount of land. It can provide urban inhabitants and school children with a new understanding and stronger connection to the production of food we need. We see these hothouses and gardens being used by individuals, restaurant owners, food pantries, recreational gardeners, educational and research institutions, and, of course, commercial hothouse farmers.

Currently, in the midst of Chicago's de facto gateways of ramping roadways, bridge underbellies and forests of columns, there are over 2,400 acres of "lost" land. This amounts to more area than all of the lakefront parks combined. Making use of this sunlit space, the proposed hothouse bridges offer a new kind of infrastructure that physically connect severed pedestrian pathways across highways while highlighting food production with a compelling crystalline architecture of growth.

We propose that 50% of these "lost" lands that cannot be built into hothouses, be planted and maintained as habitats for Chicago's itinerant dwellers; migratory birds.

(right)
Studies exploring the architectural potential of "lost" land around interchanges throughout Chicago.

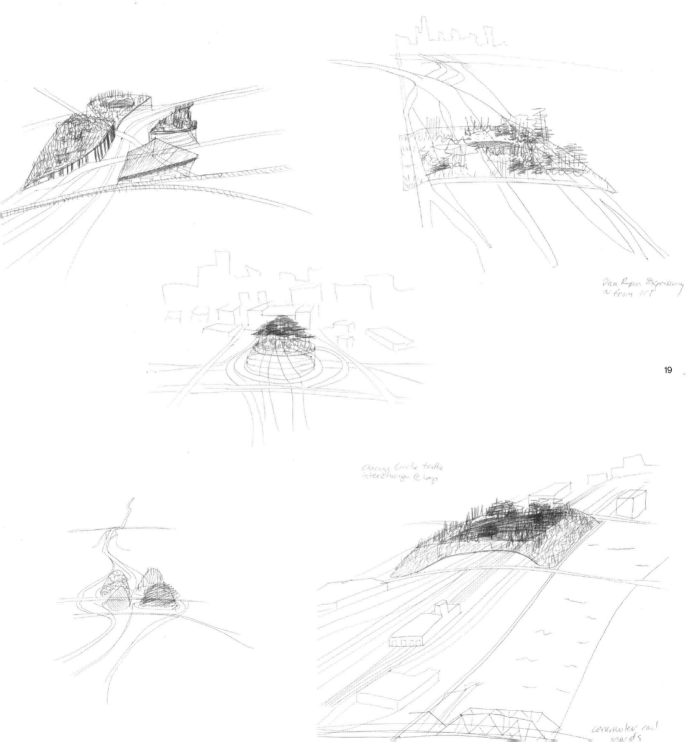

Dan Ryan Expressway
N from IIT

Chicago Circle traffic
interchange @ Congress

commuter rail
yards

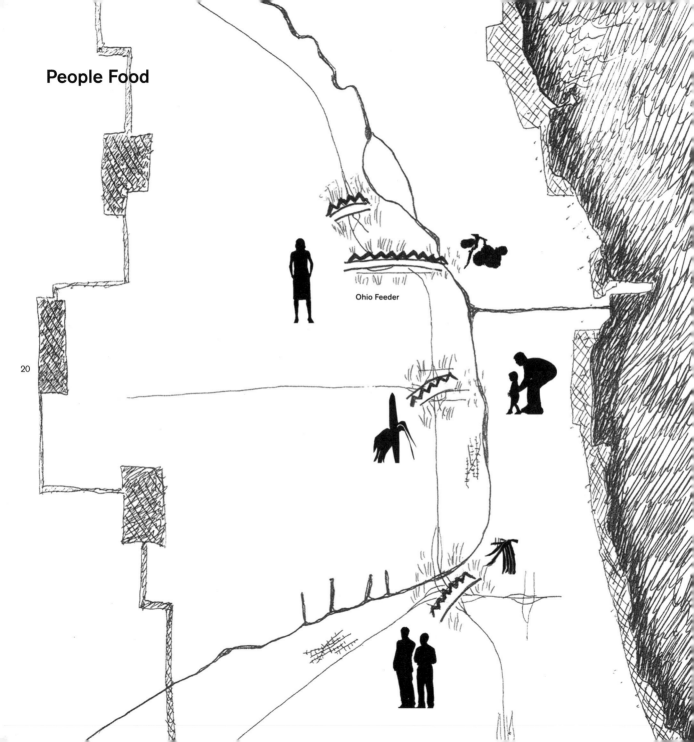

People Food

Ohio Feeder

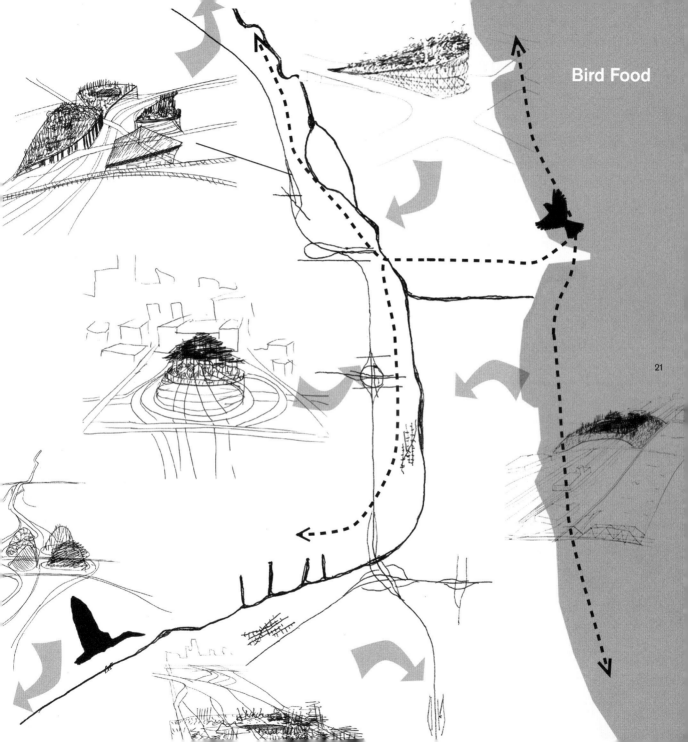

Bird Food

21

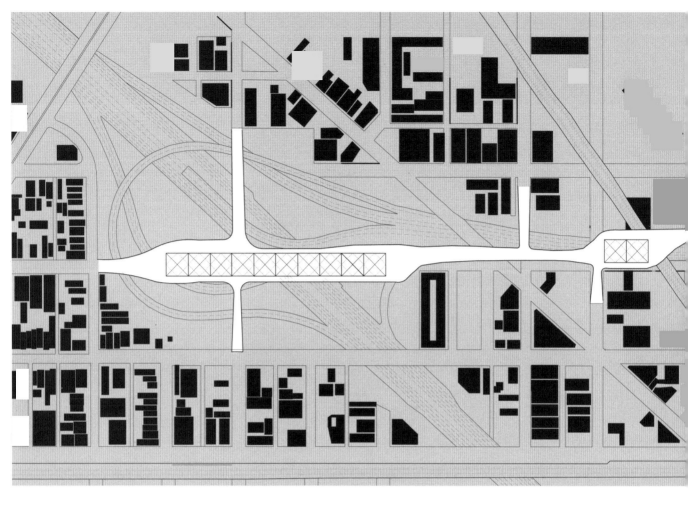

(previous)

People Food:

Hothouse food production will feed 20 families
for an entire year and at the same time reconnect
the fabric of the city.

Bird Food:

Roadway spaces provide opportunities for planting
and maintaining bird habitats transforming migration into
a bi-annual event visible at Chicago's gateways.

(above)

Site plan showing the reconnected urban fabric
across the Ohio Street Feeder ramps.

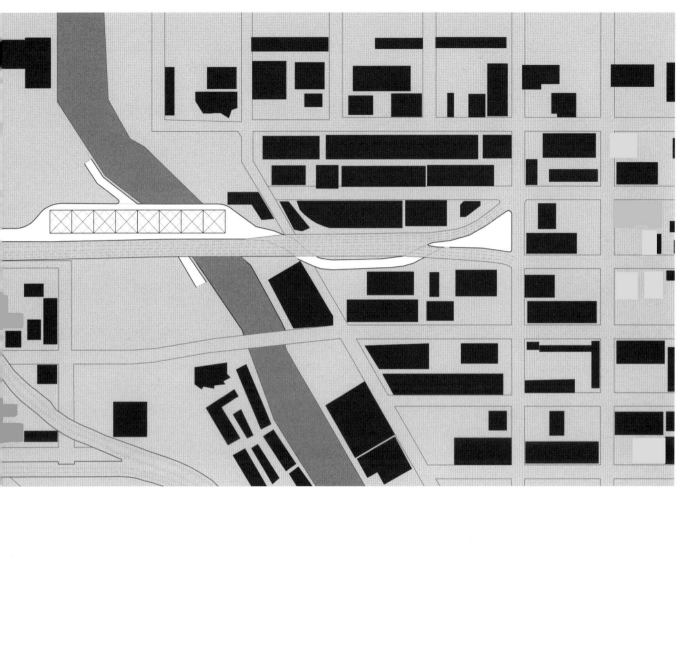

(a)

(b)

(c)

(a) A new non-automotive layer of infrastructure physically connects severed pedestrian pathways across highways.

(b) Food production is highlighted by a crystalline architecture of growth.

(c) Ohio Feeder gateway includes hothouses, gardens and landscaped areas exploiting the underutilized open space of highway interchanges.

(d) Infrastructure is often times thought of as automotive and locomotive transportation. The Ohio Feeder gateway creates a new infrastructure of food production for both people and birds.

25

GANG

I have the Ohio/Ontario gateway. This site accommodates tons of traffic and is the main entry to the City from the Ohio Street ramp. So putting program in the middle here which is also something we're looking at is really difficult because if you want retail you're not going to get foot traffic. If you want to put a restaurant, how do you get to it?
What I was trying to do was solve it – on three levels, basically, people and residential, symbol and animal. So it's a green bird stop that's the symbol.

TIGERMAN

It could be a giant birdhouse on Orleans Street. So this ramp would go up so if the trees are – full-sized trees are way up there.

It's also symbolic for Chicago in terms of this – it is really on the forefront of thinking about nature in the city and that's what Daley has been working on that I think is one of the interesting things.

GAROFALO

I think it would be interesting – I mean, I like what you're trying to do, the juxtaposition of the ecosystem in a place that you would consider it least probable.

TIGERMAN

I think it's a project the Mayor would respond to dramatically because of his environmental interests.

Since last time I started thinking about zooming out and looking at other bird resting places and migratory routes, such as the river.

TIGERMAN

I would strongly urge you to only develop the one thing.

KRUECK

A lot of us take that route all the time. It's a rather empty route. So I think to make it a richer experience from the expressway in is a – I think that would be very interesting.

GAROFALO

I think it's worth presenting the one map with all the sites and then doing the one project. The thing I'm interested in is the detail of birds and parking.

TIGERMAN

Taking care of the CO_2 emissions and stuff.

GAROFALO

Yeah. That I think is going to be a big issue.

Ohio/Ontario Gateway
Jeanne Gang

Jeanne Gang is a founding principal and a lead designer of Studio Gang Architects. Her work with Studio Gang has been internationally recognized, most recently at the Venice Biennale, as one of six firms representing the USA in the American Pavilion. The work of Studio Gang has been published widely in both National and International journals, publications, and newspapers including the New York Times, Architectural Record, the Zurich Zeitung, Blue Print Magazine, and Metropolis. She was nominated for Wired Magazine's "Rave Award" in 2004, in the field of Architecture cited as "People Changing Your Mind."

Northerly Island
Ron Krueck

Northerly Island

Sensescape is the extension of a park for Northerly Island that responds to a program for developing our perceptions of nature, and the world around us. This could not be achieved by the formalized or naturalized parks of the nineteenth and twentieth centuries, but can be achieved by Sensescape's abstractions of the essences of nature, that establish an appropriate vision for a park at the beginning of this century. These abstractions of nature would allow us to experience the essences of forests, oceans, mountains, deserts, and the Arctic, while expanding our perceptions of vision, sound, smell, taste, and touch. One could dance to the sounds of Bruce Nauman, chill out in the mists of Olafur Eliasson, or feel the spaces of James Turrell, while appreciating the Chicago skyline and the lake's edge. Sensescape's intention is to embrace and reinforce the qualities found in natural landscapes, while incorporating the city that is its backdrop, by inviting us to come and investigate these unique essences of nature. The universal abstractions of Northerly Island's Sensescape are more than a landscape. Our 21st Century inventions would instill our senses with renewed understanding of the wonders of nature, both wild and tamed.

sensescape

Experience, Perception, Consciousness, Sensibility, Taste, Smell, Hear, See, Feel

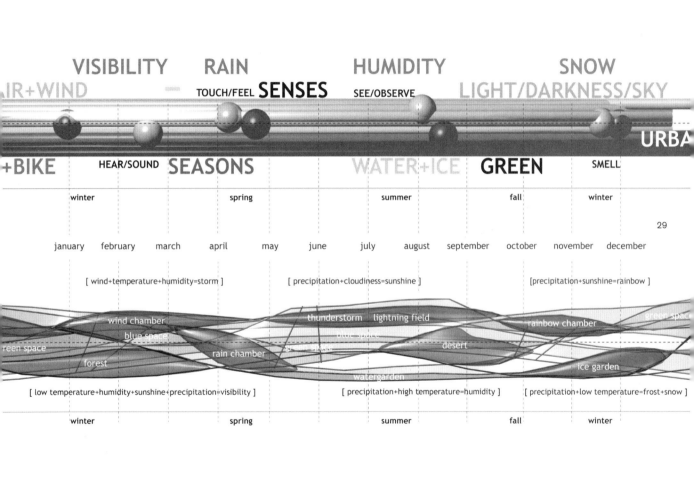

VISIBILITY   RAIN   HUMIDITY   SNOW

IR+WIND   TOUCH/FEEL **SENSES**   SEE/OBSERVE   LIGHT/DARKNESS/SKY

URBA

+BIKE   HEAR/SOUND **SEASONS**   WATER+ICE   **GREEN**   SMELL

winter   spring   summer   fall   winter

january   february   march   april   may   june   july   august   september   october   november   december

[wind+temperature+humidity=storm]   [precipitation+cloudiness=sunshine]   [precipitation+sunshine=rainbow]

wind chamber   thunderstorm   lightning field   rainbow chamber   green space

blue space   blue space

reen space   rain chamber   desert

forest   ice garden

watergarden

[low temperature+humidity+sunshine+precipitation=visibility]   [precipitation+high temperature=humidity]   [precipitation+low temperature=frost+snow]

winter   spring   summer   fall   winter

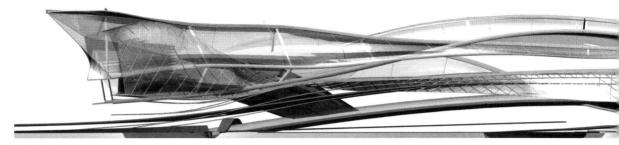

East elevation

Section structure circulation organization

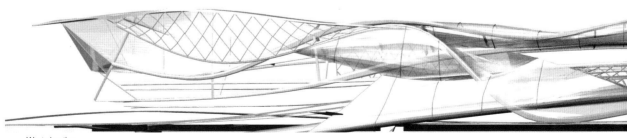

West elevation

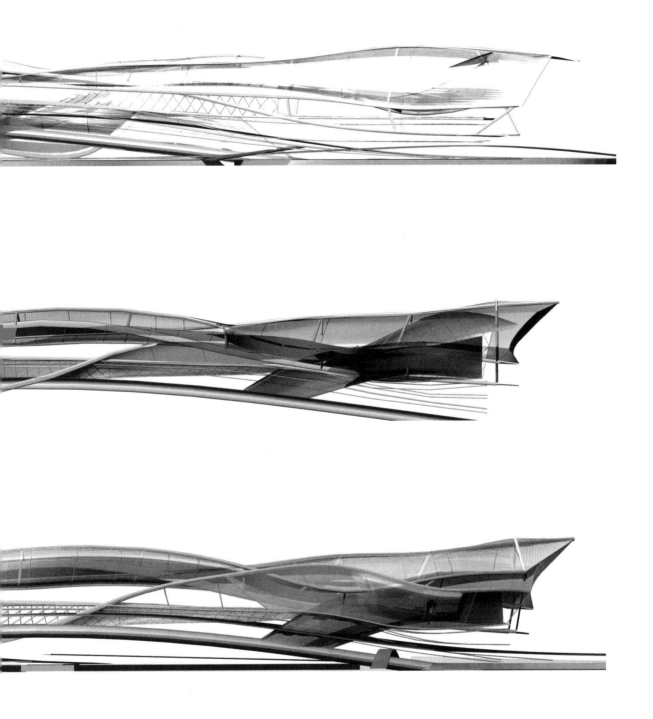

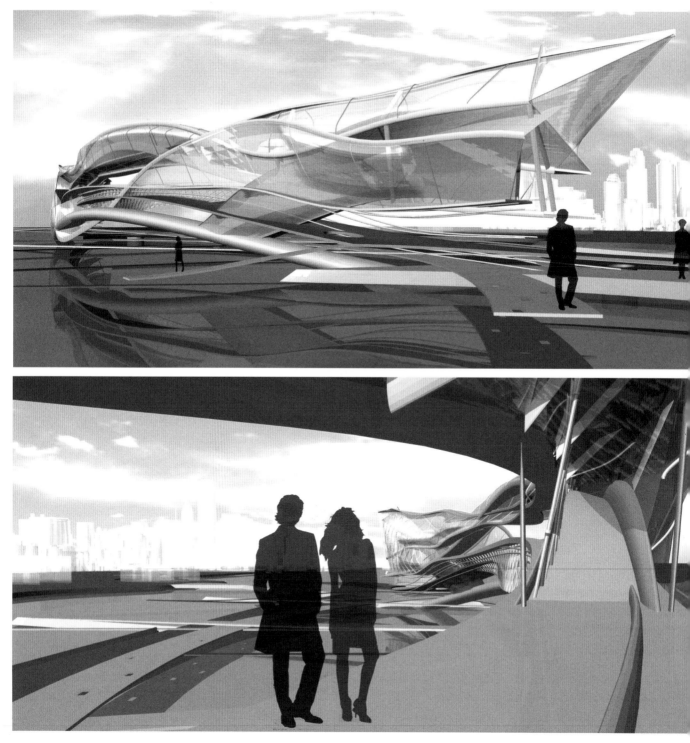

TIGERMAN
Ron was unable to be here today he is out
of the country. I'll present for him.
Ron has Northerly Island. What he is proposing
is a natatorium which is almost a vessel.
It's anchored next to a dead whale type object.
If you look at the sections it's pretty interesting.

GANG
Could I make a comment for Ron if he gets
these comments?
I've been working with these bird people and
vertical glass on the Lakefront – the birds can't
see it and they dive bomb it.

GAROFALO
Why not make it an aviary and a pool?

TIGERMAN
Yeah, that's a great idea.

GAROFALO
Why does it have to be enclosed in that point,
let the birds fly right through it.

KRUECK
**Since my last proposal I decided to
deal with it in a different way.**

TIGERMAN
Cool, I was hoping you would.

GAROFALO
It's like an ant farm. I don't know how wide it is.

**Right. I mean, I was going to call it an
ant farm, but I thought... It didn't seem
very nice.**

TIGERMAN
Been done.

**We've tried to bring the contours up
to here or maybe suppress the building a
little bit more; but when you do that it
just goes away.**

VALERIO
This vertical greenhouse with this slice into the
earth that basically emphasizes the fact that this
was a man-made island and that in that slice you
might – it might be a situation where the water
goes over you or something like that.

**It's a vertical greenhouse, and
part of it is enclosed.**

RONAN
In the formal sense I like the thing going out into
the Lake rather than running along the shoreline.
I like seeing it come down in the water.

TIGERMAN
So it becomes a jetty or a pier.

36

Northerly Island
Ron Krueck

Ron Krueck (b. 1946),
is internationally recognized
as one of the most innovative
and accomplished designers
practicing today. Since establishing his firm in 1979, he
has produced a body of work
noted for its thoughtful and
provocative explorations of
the possibilities of Modernism.
In recent years, the scale of
projects has increased, as
well as diversified with public
and institutional commissions.
Clients include such well-
known names as Spertus
Institute of Jewish Studies,
Shure, Herman Miller, Northern
Trust and Hewitt Associates.
Ron's projects have garnered
numerous design awards,
including 17 National and
Chicago Chapter AIA Design
Awards, an AIA Top Ten Green
Project and a National Building
Award for steel construction.
Ron is a member of the Interior
Design Hall of Fame.

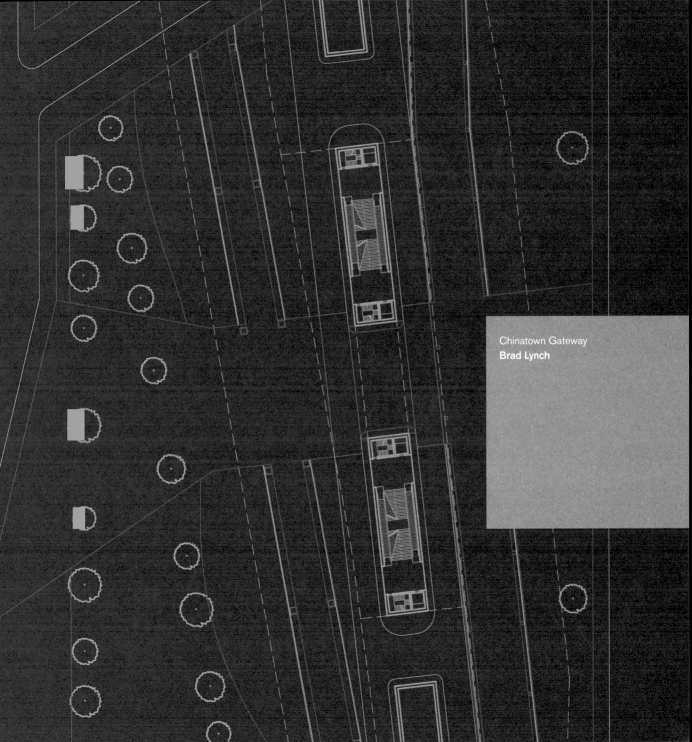

Chinatown Gateway
Brad Lynch

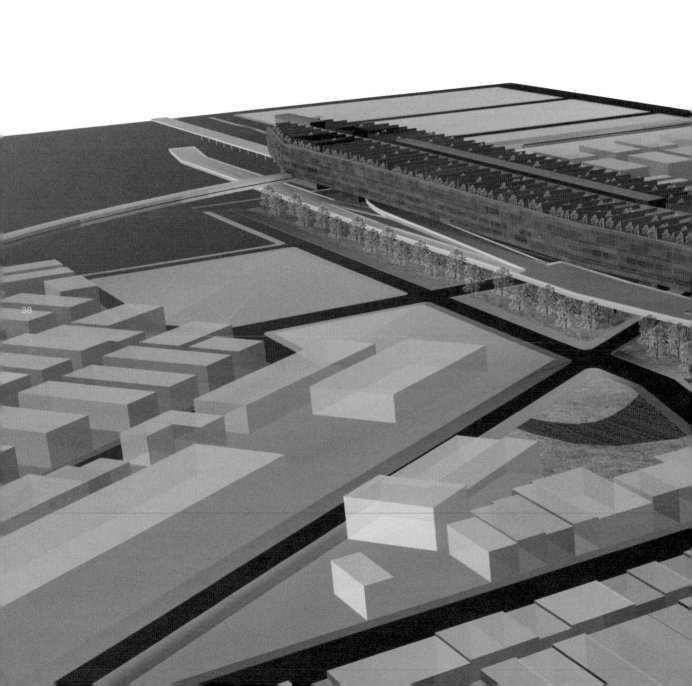

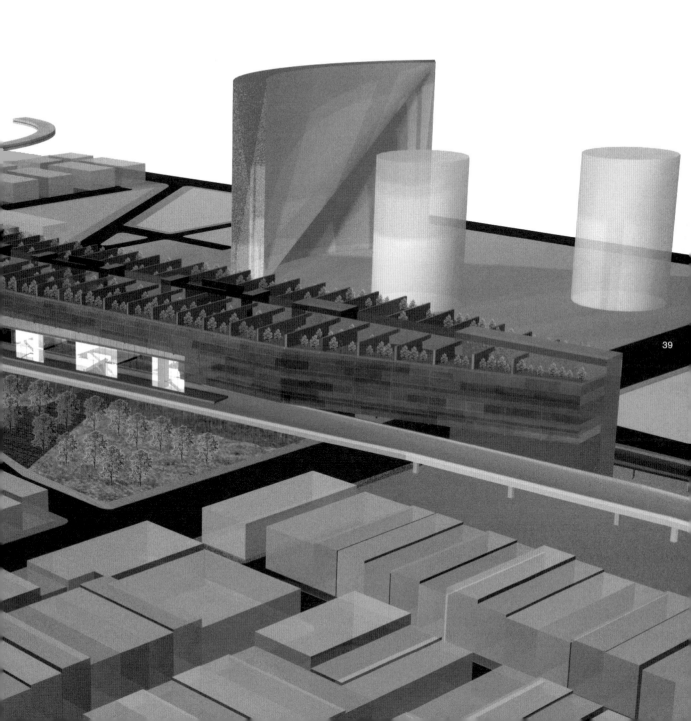

A tangle of roadways, rail lines, and other infrastructures currently isolates Chinatown from its surroundings. To make a visual and functional gateway to the area, we propose a lantern-like transportation hub that will combine CTA trains, bus routes, and Metra into a centralized mass that also contains retail, markets, restaurants, and parking for over 3,500 cars. The Chinatown Gateway addresses the neighborhood's potential as a transportation hub and portal to the Loop and McCormick Place, while emphasizing Chinatown's status as a cultural destination.

The position of the gateway structure entails numerous changes in infrastructure planning. These include the relocation of the entrance to the Dan Ryan expressway on axis with Clark Street; the realignment of Wentworth Avenue as it crosses Cermak Road; the elimination of two travel lanes on both Archer Avenue and Cermak Road; and the addition of a green, pedestrian walkway that connects the traditional retail area on Wentworth to Ping Tom Park and creates a view corridor to the Loop. These changes seek to maintain and emphasize the identity of central Chinatown while encouraging low-density development to the south and west. The Gateway building is a version of a cable-stayed structure. Poured-in-place

concrete cores support a structural system of pre-cast, post-tensioned concrete elements that hang over the rail lines (most of which would remain unchanged). Translucent, cast-concrete panels hang at the perimeter of the structure, admitting natural light into parking and market areas, while lending the structure a lantern-like quality at night. Rooftop gardens feature patios for dining and public seating; interspersed openings in the roof that provide natural light and ventilation to the market and parking below.

(pages 38-39)
Aerial view of Chinatown Gateway, looking Northeast

(left)
West facade of Chinatown Gateway as seen from the Southwest corner at Wentworth and Cermak

(below)
Tree lined pathway that leads to Ping Tom Park

(a) Train entrance and public area
(b) Fourth floor market area:
    Flexible booth and panel systems direct
    natural light and ventilation. Individual areas
    can be expanded or contracted.
(c) "El" platform
(d) Roof terrace:
    Planting areas are interspersed with openings
    for natural light and ventilation and for seating
    areas for public and restaurant use.
(e) Section looking North

(next page)
West elevation and main entrance

(e)

LYNCH

I didn't know what gateway meant, but when I started investigating this my gateway became 200 acres when looking at Chinatown. I've ignored all of the development and planning north of Wentworth Avenue for the last ten years.

GANG
Did you tear my building down?
Yes, I did.

GANG
It's just opening up.
We're going to move it over.

GANG
It's a community center, come on.
So what I'm looking at doing in terms of the basic problem, is hooking all the transportation together and creating a parking structure. The idea is that once you arrive there you can either, as a pedestrian, go to the market place, the transportation hub, to residential or pick up the shuttle bus.

GAROFALO
I think a problem that I don't know if you solved is Cermak Road – that road is just death.

TIGERMAN
Who the hell could do this, this sort of research? It's a side of you that I never saw.

The last time I presented you may remember that I took the Robert Moses approach of nuking Chinatown.

GANG
You better not tear down my building
So I'm leaving everything and just tearing down your building. It took a long time for me to come up with anything on this in terms of thinking what – kind of what the big idea would be for the gateway.

TIGERMAN
How long is the building?
It's like 1800 feet.

TIGERMAN
I think it's a very thought-through scheme...

WOODHOUSE
So having created all this parking in the building, what happens to the parking that's now on the ground?
That all becomes green space. So if you look at the green against this, this goes up and adjoins to the park up there. There's a lot of other technical things we're looking at adding with the translucent concrete, but also in the glass areas, laminated glass for LED screens for the displays.

Chinatown Gateway
Brad Lynch

Brad Lynch is a principal with Brininstool + Lynch, which he co-founded in 1989 with David Brininstool. In the past fifteen years, the firm has received fourteen Design Excellence Awards from the American Institute of Architects - Chicago, an American Architecture Award, and was honored as an Emerging Voice in architecture by the Architectural League of New York in 2003. Their work has been regularly published in journals and magazines and they have been included in recent books on architecture and design. In addition, two monographs have been published on the firm, the most recent being, *Brininstool + Lynch, Building on Modernism*, from Edizioni Press.

with
Eirik Agustsson
Mareny de Campos
Jerico Prater

46

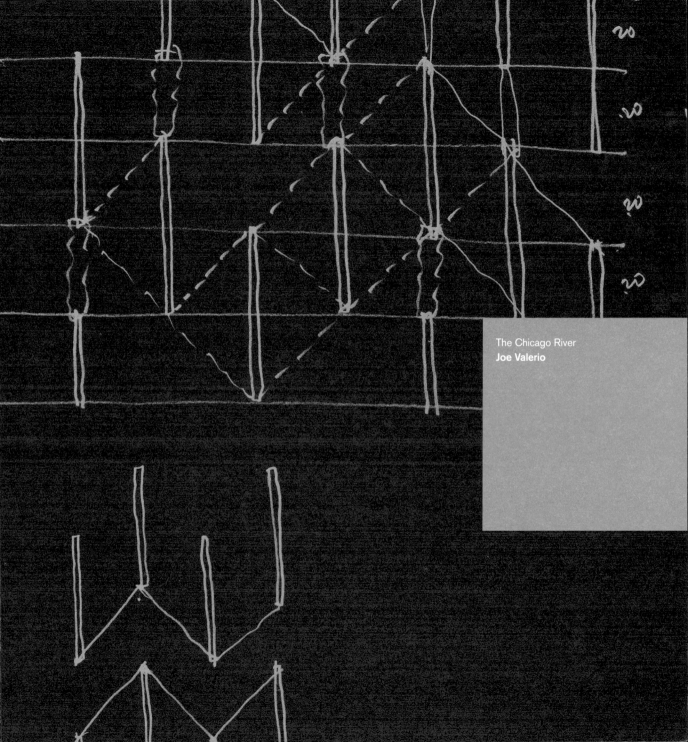

The Chicago River
Joe Valerio

Musée de L'eau

The Lake

Empty and vast, Lake Michigan is a blank place. It is without features, without a memory of what it is, what it was and what it will be. It is shaped by a complex system that we do not fully understand, and its shape changes from moment to moment. After these moments it returns to a state of rest, a state where its vast blankness is relentless.

The River

Upside down is the condition of the Chicago River. Once upon a time it flowed from the low swamp that is Chicago into Lake Michigan. One day, the people of the City decided to turn the river upside down and reverse its flow.
It begins where it shouldn't and leads where it couldn't in a ballet choreographed by civil engineers.

The Intersection

Edges are filled with energy. The Chicago River is an edge that divides the City. It is enigmatic, the other side is obscure and uncertain. The lakeshore is an edge that separates the known from the unknown. It is ambiguous, the meaning of the lake is never clear nor fully understood. The intersection of these two edges, one enigmatic and the other ambiguous, explains more about Chicago as a place than any other point in the City.

The Structure

Nothing marks the intersection of these two edges, it is an anonymous place. The tensegrity frame makes a place out of nowhere. Its square plan celebrates the river and the lake making a space out of the place these two lines cross on the map. The tensegrity frame is visually tenuous. The beams and columns are not continuous, instead they are held in place by a network of cables. The choreography of the structure embraces the energy where these two edges collide.

The Locks

Damming the lake, the structure holds back its waters, defining a square basin. The water level in the basin is controlled by two locks whose operation raises or lowers the water level in the basin, allowing ships to move from Lake to River and back.

The Museum

Water slips through your fingers. It is a substance whose form is always changing. Like air, it is always there and always in the background. The Musée de L'eau, will move water from the background to the foreground, celebrating water as a surface, as a habitat, and as a cultural icon.

48

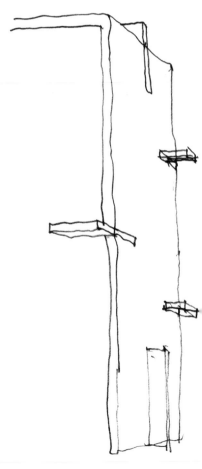

(above)
The museum entrance faces south towards Grant Park.

(above)
A boat approaches from the Lake, both locks are closed.
The lakeside lock opens to allow the boat to enter the basin.
The lock itself is a large platform that people can ride.
The boat moves towards the riverside lock while the level
of the water in the basin drops.
The riverside lock opens and the boat moves upriver.

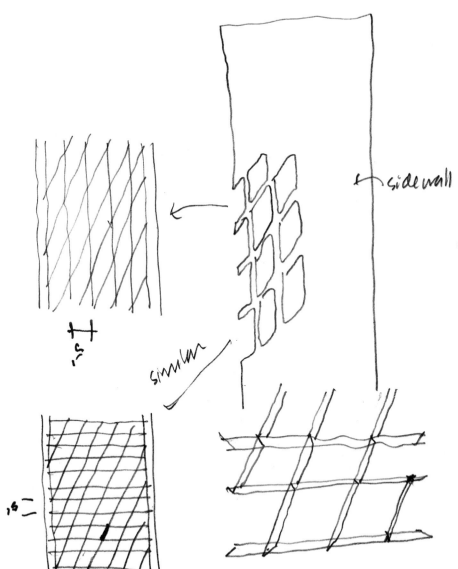

sidewall

51

similar

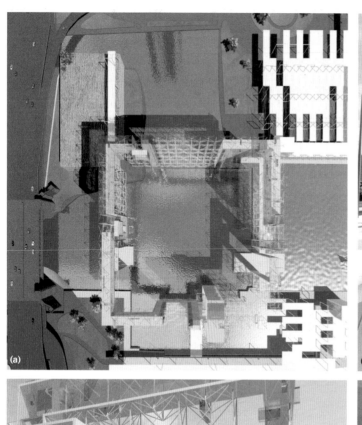

(previous)

(a) Aerial perspective of the museum and the lock basin.

(b) The museum structure as it snakes across the sky is supported by a tensegrity frame.

(c) The waterspout at the museum entrance celebrates the importance of water to the City.

(d) Interior view of the museum looking towards Navy Pier and the Lake.

(e) From overhead the intersection of the River and the edge of the lakefront is marked by the new square basin.

(f) The museums collection includes not only artifacts from the lake, and a geological history of the region, but also animal and plant specimens which depend on this eco-system for survival.

(g) Looking through the tensegrity frame toward downtown Chicago.

(h) With Navy Pier in the background, the new museum dominates the view from the Lake Shore Drive bridge

(below)

Musée de L'eau and the new Chicago locks from the lake. The new events structures appear to the right and left of the main basin.

VALERIO

To me the fuzziest part of Chicago's lakefront is the point at which the river actually starts. There ought to be something here that really takes something that's anonymous and makes it a memorable experience.

TIGERMAN

So when it becomes vertical, this thing, then the fabric will, albeit while lifted up, you can walk under the structure.

Correct, and it becomes a windbreak, a protected area.

GAROFALO

So the ends are like beaches almost.

Yeah, it's like a fabric beach.

LYNCH

So what is the pedestrian use?

You keep asking me those detailed questions. The thought was it's that crossing point, that intersection between the River and the Lakefront, you know, a gathering place.

GAROFALO

I like that it's something that is kind of new and foreign material other than, say, bricks and mortar.

RONAN

I think it's an object but if you continue it, it's a strategy.

Let me switch seats with you Ron, only because Stanley, I assume, has the weakest eyes here.

TIGERMAN

Why because I'm the oldest?

Yeah.

My scheme started out looking at the locks, then the whole thing transitioned into a museum about water.

So the notion has become the idea of creating a square structure 400 feet on the side and 200 feet high, which defines a ring that separates the Lake level from the lower River level.

TIGERMAN

So they become the locks or something?

Yeah, and there are two bridges that cross the structure at water level and when they raise and lower they are also the lock gates. The interior of the structure is a museum.

TIGERMAN

The entrapped body of water is the up and down.

GAROFALO

I keep thinking – I thought what you were going to do is have the water raise up inside the cube while people were on the perimeter as kind of an engineering demonstration.

Well, that's interesting. We did talk about having one flooded with water.

The Chicago River
Joe Valerio

Joseph Valerio received his Bachelor of Architecture from the University of Michigan, and a Master of Architecture degree from U.C.L.A. In 1970, he began working with Chrysalis Corp. Architects, which took an interdisciplinary approach to design, teaming architects with artists and scientists. The group participated in the EAT (Experiments in Art and Technology) project for Pepsi-Cola at Expo 70 in Osaka. In 1973, he began teaching at the University of Wisconsin-Milwaukee's School of Architecture and Urban Planning, becoming an Associate Professor in 1979. He also founded C.O.W. (Chrysalis of Wisconsin), winning his first National AIA Honor Award in 1981. He returned to Chicago in 1985, working as Vice President for Architecture at A. Epstein & Sons before starting his own firm, Valerio-Associates, Inc. in 1988. In 1994, Valerio-Associates, Inc. merged with another Chicago firm, Train Dewalt Associates.

with
Kyle Reynolds
Jeff Mikolajewski

Visualization Studies:
Thorsten Bosch
Visualized Concepts

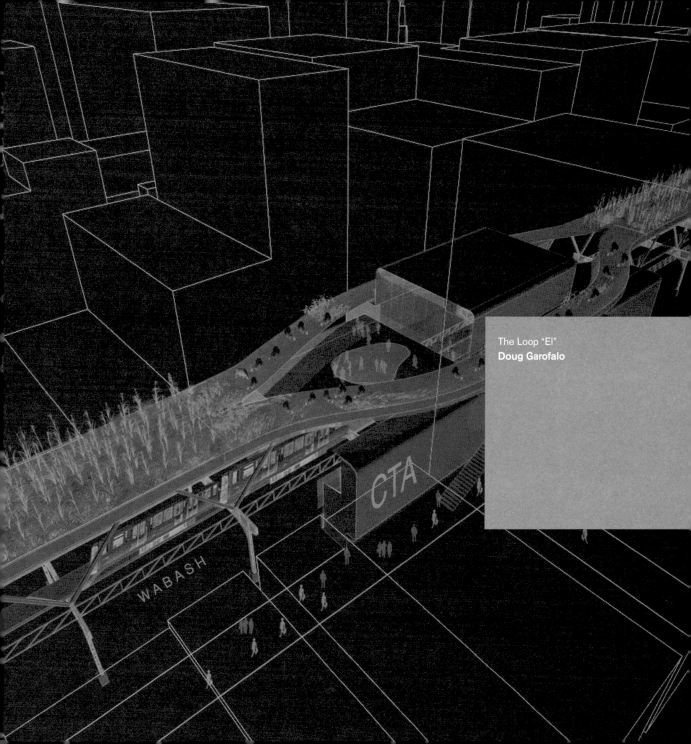

The Loop "El"
Doug Garofalo

(below)
An Agricultural Plateau is placed over all the elevated
train tracks in the loop, and a series of station modifica-
tions introduce institutional and cultural destinations.

(a) Existing "El" Structure
(b) New Loop Agricultural Plateau
(c) Access from State Street
(d) New AIC School of Art, Design and Technology
(e) New Home of Chicago Office of Tourism
(f) Wabash sidewalk Arcade
(g) New Home for Chicago Architecture Foundation
(h) Renovated Stations with street level Arcades

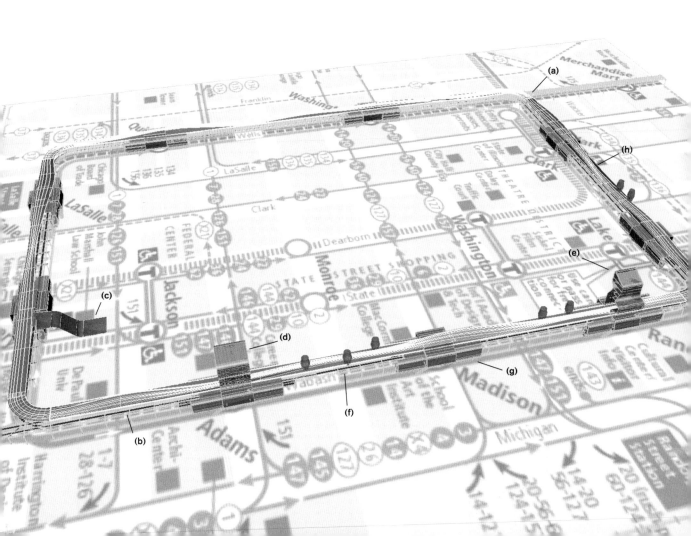

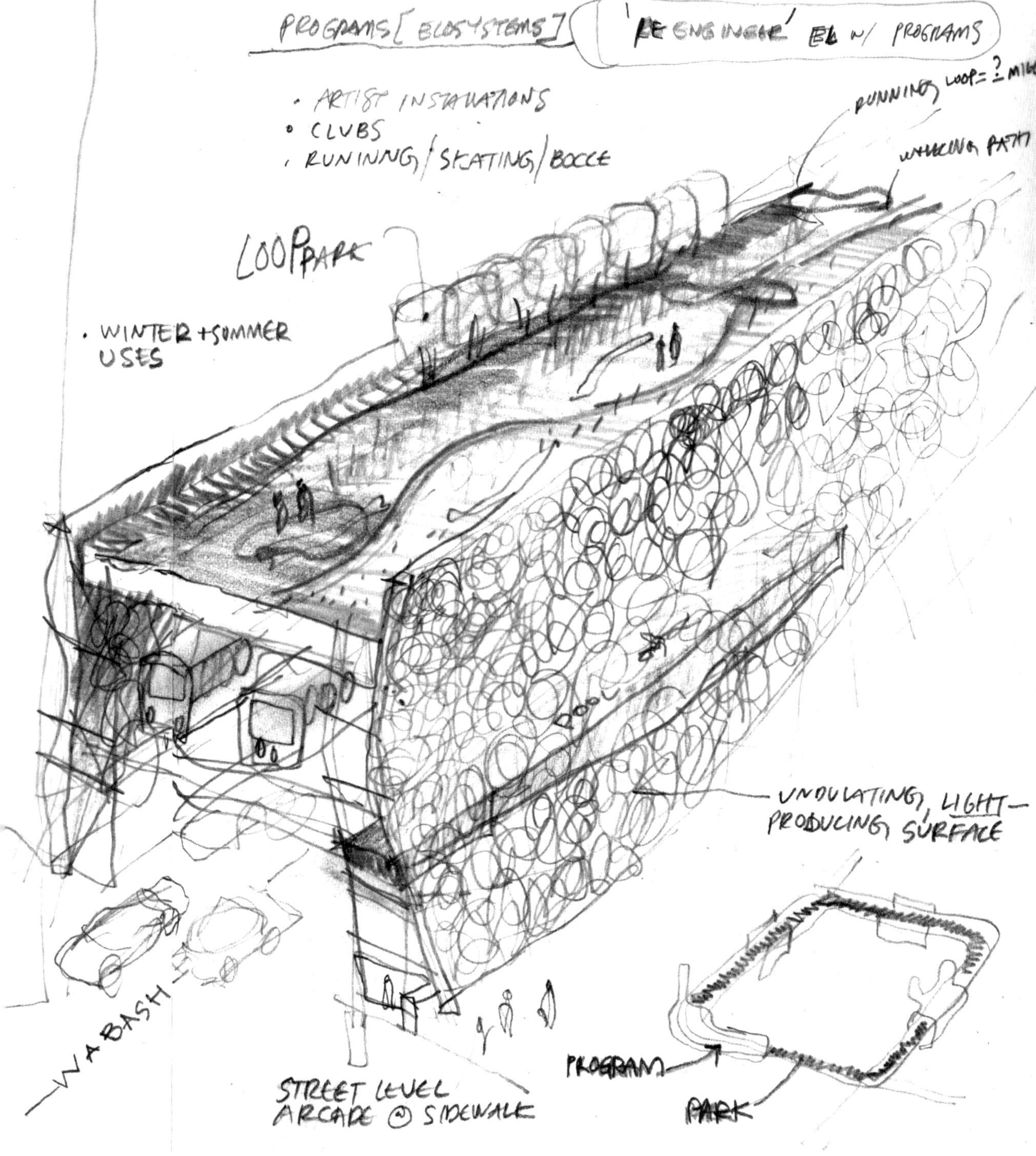

PROGRAMS [ECOSYSTEMS]   'RE-ENGINEER' EL w/ PROGRAMS

· ARTIST INSTALLATIONS
· CLUBS
· RUNNING / SKATING / BOCCE

LOOP PARK

· WINTER + SUMMER USES

RUNNING LOOP = ? MILES
WALKING PATH

UNDULATING, LIGHT-PRODUCING SURFACE

WABASH

STREET LEVEL ARCADE @ SIDEWALK

PROGRAM

PARK

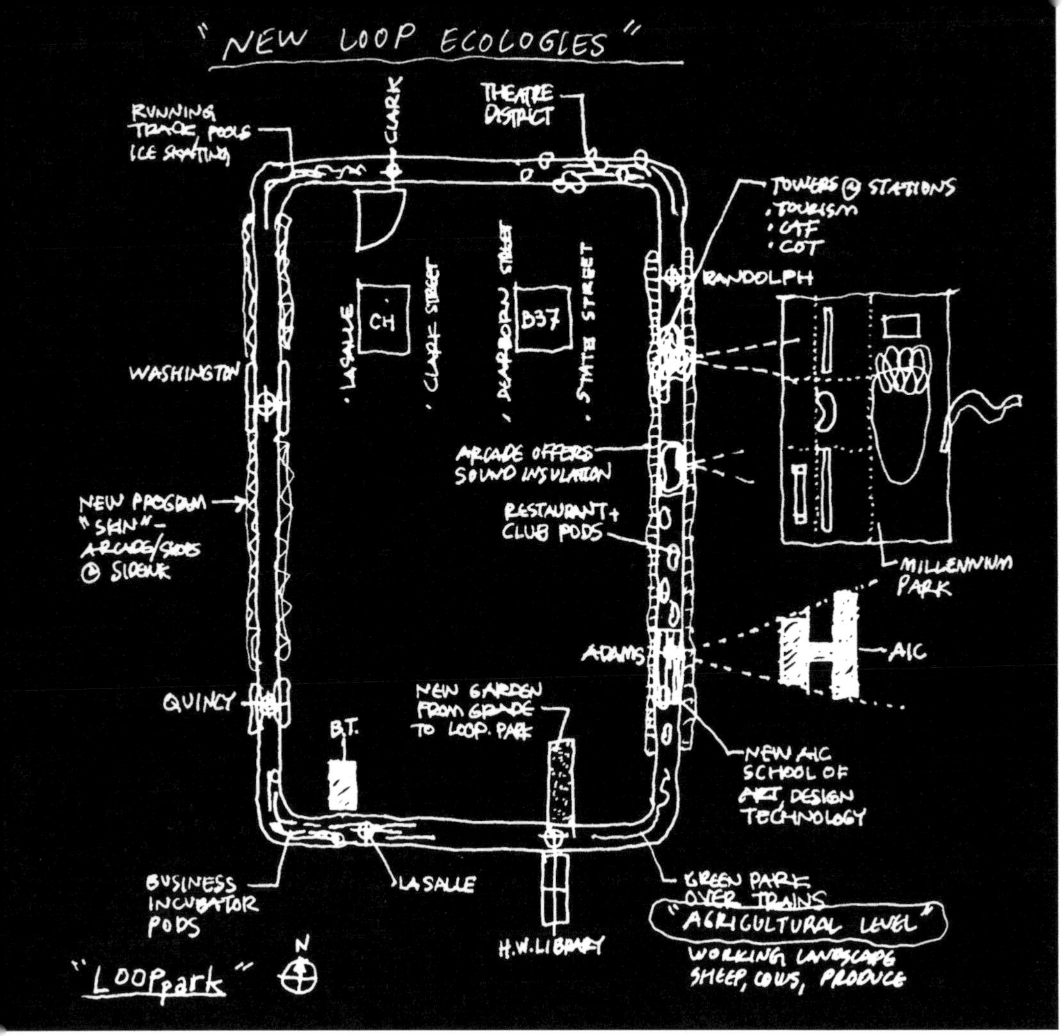

"NEW LOOP ECOLOGIES"

RUNNING TRACK, POOLS ICE SKATING

CLARK

THEATRE DISTRICT

TOWERS @ STATIONS
. TOURISM
. CAF
. COT

RANDOLPH

LA SALLE
CH
CLARK STREET
DEARBORN STREET
D37
SMITH STREET

WASHINGTON

ARCADE OFFERS SOUND INSULATION

RESTAURANT + CLUB PODS

MILLENNIUM PARK

NEW PROGRAM "SKIN" - ARCADE/SHOPS @ SIDEWK

QUINCY

B.T.

NEW GARDEN FROM GRADE TO LOOP. PARK

ADAMS

H

AIC

NEW AIC SCHOOL OF ART, DESIGN TECHNOLOGY

BUSINESS INCUBATOR PODS

LA SALLE

GREEN PARK OVER TRAINS

"AGRICULTURAL LEVEL"

H.W. LIBRARY

WORKING LANDSCAPE SHEEP, COWS, PRODUCE

"LOOPpark"   N

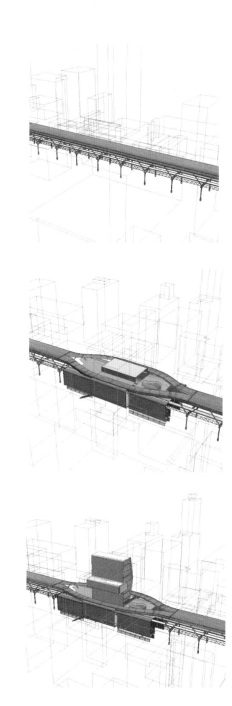

61

(left)
The proposed enhancements to the "El" are meant to
transform the antiquated industrial system into a new
composite of surfaces and landscapes.

(right)
Three various prototypical station improvements.
The Agricultural Plateau combines with various programs
at each entry point to the elevated train system.

DRINK

(left)
The Agricultural Plateau is a productive landscape of edible
plants and animals that serve the new sidewalk arcades below.
Visual access to this landscape for the general public is from
new entertainment and institutional towers centered over the
existing station stops.

(below)
The new Agricultural Plateau offers bucolic views to
weary office workers in the loop.

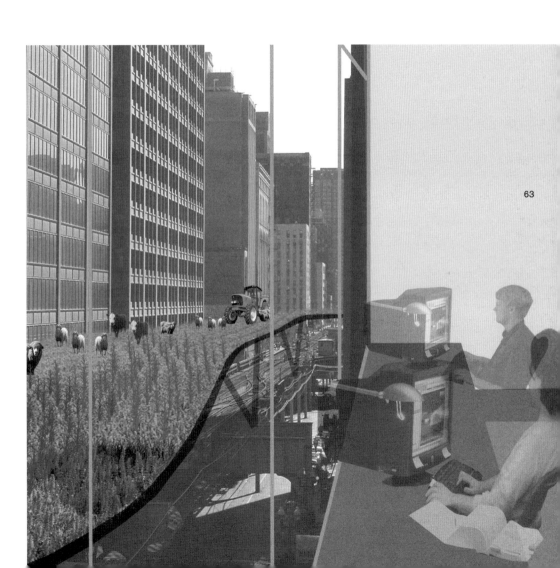

63

New Loop Ecologies

Of all cities, Chicago must not cleanse away its toughness. As it greens, cleans and otherwise improves itself, it must not sanitize itself to the point of homogeneity. The Loop elevated train system, that tangle of steel and noise and rust is one of the defining moments of downtown; instead of burying this important piece of infrastructure (like Boston), it is here seen as a scaffold to support additional programs. These programs are manifold and take the form of new station stops outfitted with public activities combined with a new and continuous rooftop ecology.

Programmed Stations

This proposal envisions a new system of "El" stations that are site specifically programmed with a variety of institutions and activities. Public oriented programs such as the Chicago Office of Tourism and the Chicago Architecture Foundation are seen as small tower structures that hover over appropriate intersections. At street level is a contemporary arcade that also forms an insulating barrier between street, "El" structure and pedestrian. Between the arcade and the towers stretching alongside the tracks are various linear functions such as swimming, bocce ball, exhibition halls, express bicycle lanes, and other such spaces where sound is not an issue.

Agricultural Plateau

While it is tempting to add to Chicago's increasingly rich system of recreational parks, this proposal envisions a working, self-sufficient agricultural landscape over the entire system of train tracks as defined by the Loop. Actual public access is limited in favor of producing fields of consumer crops and foliage crops (for animals). These would consist primarily of corn and soy beans, with additional, smaller patches of Alliums, Brassicas, Greens, Herbs, Fruiting and Root crops. This new field is inhabited mainly by sheep and goats, which produce milk, cheese and wool.

SWIM

FRESH PRODUCE

CTA

GAROFALO
I'm proposing a system for the "El" to densify the tracks and envelope them with program to abate noise, but also to bring activity to the street.
The skin turns into a light source and emanates a certain kind of light, artificial light.

TIGERMAN
Harry Weese did some stuff on the "El" in the 50's and 60's and what your doing is much more complex.
And I think it's a system that can envelope the "El" just as kind of a tube or a blanket of program. It can also start to sprout larger programs, like towers or midrise buildings, slivers that would be between the corridors of Wabash.

LYNCH
I wouldn't get rid of the noise though. It's one of the only places in the city where actually the sound is part of the experience.

GANG
Did you ever notice why people in Chicago talk so loud. They're half deaf. I'm losing it from the Blue Line.

LYNCH
The disappointing part is that the stations are really lackluster. I mean they're big disappointments.

TIGERMAN
The lackluster thing is not just Chicago. The whole BART system in San Francisco, though modern for its time, were really pretty lackluster.

GANG
So are you going to go more into one location and just have some detailed programming?
I think we have to show one in even more detail than this to have it make sense.

VALERIO
Doug, couldn't that also – if it occurred at a cross street, it would be this kind of like punctuation mark?

GAROFALO
We're in the process of going all the way around the loop and trying to be very specific – and really scrutinize these things and make them site-specific as opposed to saying we're going to put a tower at every stop.
We're going to figure out, you know, like if the Chicago Marathon were to be run through the Loop it would take a detour up here and then come back down.

TIGERMAN
Around the park. Run around the park above the "El"
There would be a running track for sure up there.

TIGERMAN
So that you do get light, but that you still could run along the continuous thing.
Cool. That would be worthwhile.

The Loop "El"
Doug Garofalo

Garofalo is currently a Professor at the University of Illinois Chicago School of Architecture, where he served as Acting Director from 2001-2003. In 2001 Garofalo was selected for the "Emerging Voices" program at the Architectural League of New York, was featured as "The New Vanguaurd" for *Architectural Record*, and had speculative work included in the "Folds, Blobs and Boxes" exhibit at the Carnegie Museum in Pittsburgh. In 1995 he won the AIA Chicago Young Architect Award, and in 1991 was the recipient of a Young Architect Award given by The Architectural League of New York based on the theme of "Practice." He received a Master's degree from Yale University in 1987, and was awarded the prestigious Skidmore Owings & Merrill Foundation Traveling Fellowship.

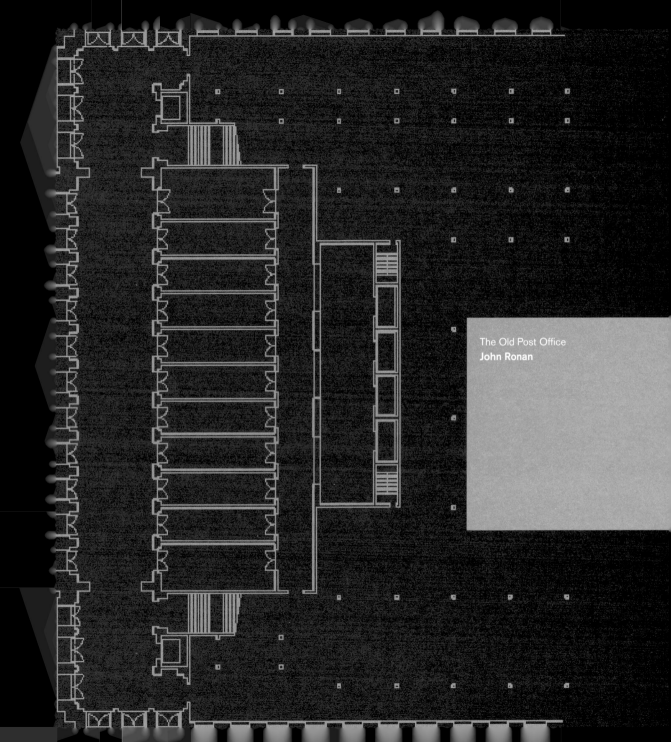

The Old Post Office
John Ronan

(a)

(b)

(a) The funeral cortege disembarks and ascends
    an incline to large rusting steel doors that lead to
    the Remembrance Hall.
(b) Funeral barges approach the river landing.
(c) The Old Post Office is re-programmed as an
    urban burial site, initiating a new funeral ritual via
    the river that becomes unique to Chicago.
(d) The deep floor plates and existing structure allow
    crypts and niches to be stacked six high,
    accommodating over 90,000 plots per floor.

69

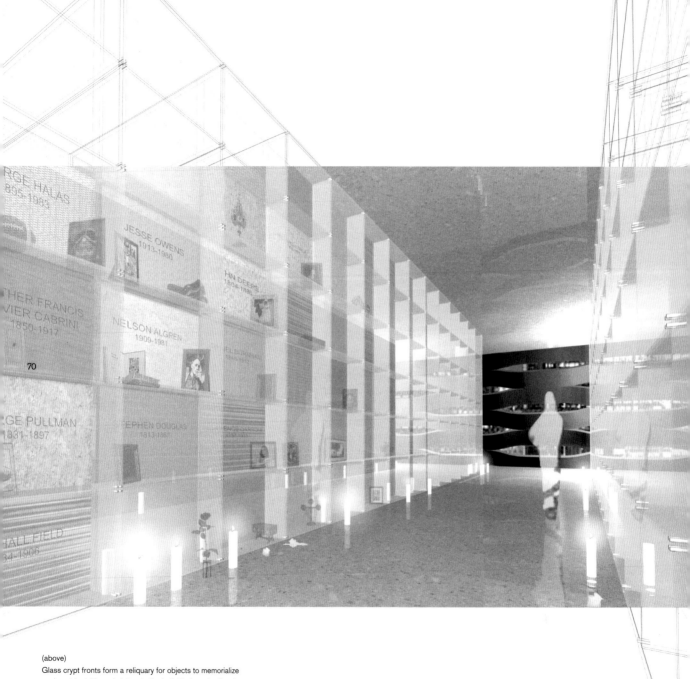

70

(above)

Glass crypt fronts form a reliquary for objects to memorialize
each resident. Viewed obliquely, the individual crypts dissolve
into a single reflective plane. Holes in the floor receive votive
candles and flowers brought by visitors.

The Old Post Office

A funeral barge floats silently down the Chicago River to the site where the Old Post Office once stood. A figure clad in white steps onto the river landing, and leads those gathered at the river's edge up an incline to the foot of the large, rusting steel doors. The figure knocks. A hollow echo precedes the slow opening of the doors to reveal a long hall lined on one side with chapels. The white figure leads the group to the open chapel where the ritual of life and death takes place. The rear wall of the chapel opens wide, leading the funeral party to the crypts above. Upstairs, the funeral procession winds through the glass crypts, past the reliquaries that hold souvenirs of lives now past. The reflection of candle flames flicker in the polished floor, animating the wind that passes through the open facade. As mourners file away to the rooftop garden to look out over the city, the white figure lingers. Currently, Chicago devotes over 78 million square feet of land to cemeteries that are becoming increasingly overcrowded as our population ages – around 24,000 people die in Chicago each year; by 2060 the number is projected to be 36,000. As the city gets denser and land pressures increase, we will be forced to rethink, as a society, how we remember our fellow citizens. Because of its size, configuration and structural capacity, the Old Post Office suggests itself for re-programming as a new urban cemetery, able to honor Chicagoans for the next 100 years.

71

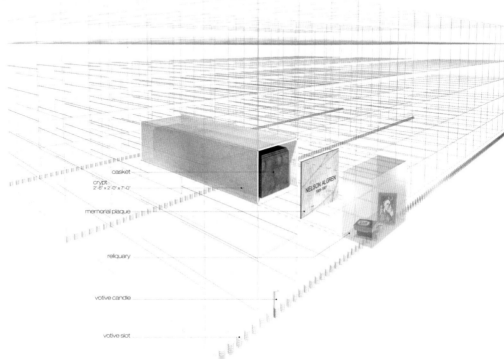

casket

crypt
2'-6" x 2'-0' x 7'-0"

memorial plaque

reliquary

votive candle

votive slot

NELSON ALGREN

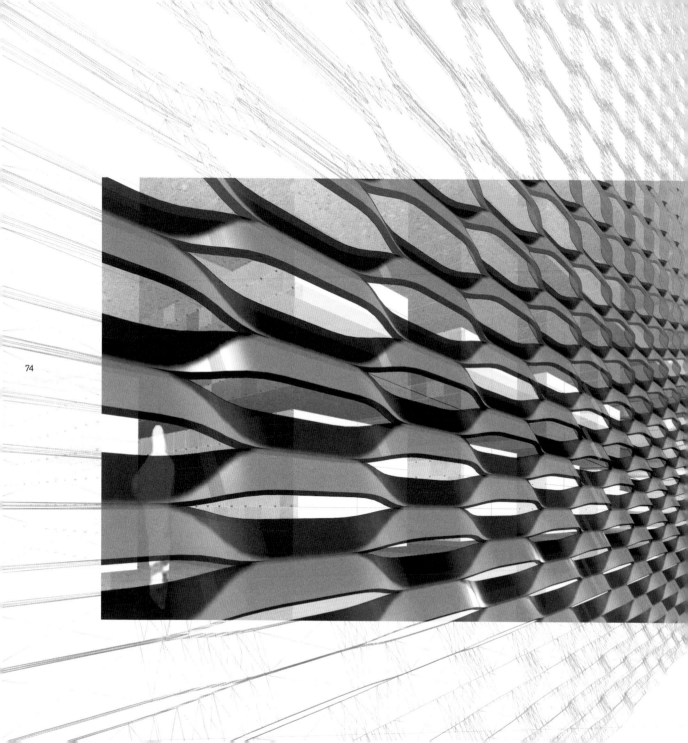

An open-air skin allows light and air
to filter into the crypt levels.

(right)
Rusting steel panels clad the roadway
passage through the building.
Cars emerge into the light at either end.

75

RONAN

The idea in a nutshell is turn the post office into a municipal cemetery and empty out existing cemeteries in the city and use the land as parks.

The idea here is to kind of use this location on the river as some form of ritual that could kind of have a funeral barge taking people to the post office. So a ritual in Chicago would evolve around this.

TIGERMAN

This is a great image. It's something picturesque about death.

Sign me up. I want to be buried there.

GANG

Is it just for the unclaimed?

No. It's for anybody who wanted to be buried in the City of Chicago.

GANG

John, can I ask you what the dead load is on the floor?

GAROFALO

I don't know that you need to clear out the existing cemeteries to make the project viable.

TIGERMAN

This is probably, as Brad says, by far and away the most economically believable use of a building that you could ever possibly imagine.

Well, what do you think? How important is the vacating of the old cemeteries?

TIGERMAN

I think you're just complicating it.

GAROFALO

It's also interesting to think about the public space implications. There is this guy from Florida, I can't think of his name, Gregory Ulmer, I think. He wrote a lot about mourning and did some memorial designs for architects and he's got this interesting set of ideas for what he calls electronic monumentality where you can see images of loved ones at these sacred places.

KRUECK

I have one question as an image of a gateway into the city, I mean it's a major gateway.

TIGERMAN

It's a question of how much in a state of denial one is.

KRUECK

I just brought it up.

TIGERMAN

No. It went through all of our minds when he first presented it, but it's a very potent scheme. I think it's very poetic, I think you should talk about it or anticipate it anyway.

The Old Post Office
John Ronan

John Ronan graduated with a Master of Architecture with distinction from the Harvard University Graduate School of Design in 1991, where he was awarded the Julia Amory Appleton Traveling Fellowship, after completing a Bachelor of Science with honors from the University of Michigan. He established a practice in Chicago in 1997, John Ronan Architect, which has built projects ranging in scale from houses to large public buildings. He was a winner in the Townhouse Revisited Competition staged by the Graham Foundation in 1999 and winner of the prestigious Perth Amboy High School Design Competition in 2004, a 471,000 square foot high school to be built in New Jersey. In December 2000, he was named as a member of the Design Vanguard by *Architectural Record* magazine, and his work has been featured in numerous publications and journals. He is currently an Assistant Professor at the Illinois Institute of Technology College of Architecture, where he has taught since 1992.

with
Micah Land

South Loop Educational District
David Woodhouse

A Project for the
Education District

Chicago's immense horizontal grid is abstracted in a hovering net, suspended high above its streets as a silvery reticulated plane that bounds/integrates/animates the city's densest concentration of institutions of higher learning. The net's expanse floats (allowing the city to be the city) as it intensifies the urban campus paradigm by transforming the streets into a campus where Chicago itself is the heart of the curriculum. It works at city scale and pedestrian scale, from the streets below and the towers above, in the narrow Wabash canyon and the sprawl of low buildings and parking lots in the South Loop, all day and all night, to define the fourteen-block Education District (Jackson to 11th, State to Michigan) with its eleven colleges and universities, 37,000 students and 10,000 faculty members. A rectilinear web of cables, suspended from tapered columns, holds panels of programmable LED nodes and the photovoltaic cells that power them. By day, its reticulated strands define spaces, filter views and etch a shimmering screen across sky and skyscrapers, casting a delicate tracery of shadows on the streets below. At night, the net's arrays of multicolored ever-changing LEDs are pixels in a city sized-video screen. Artists create kinetic lightscapes measuring three Sears Towers in length and students improvise light riffs by "playing" the net's LEDs from interactive keyboard consoles and city info-kiosks. The net is a Chicago-scale place-maker, connecting/meshing/wiring the Education District with gleaming-in-the-sunshine changing to pulsing-with-bright-lights urban land art.

(a) 55' tall x 30" diameter at base
    Type 316 stainless steel column -
    taper column at 1650' radius
(b) 2" diameter 6 x 32
    Type 316 stainless steel cable on
    10' x 10' grid, 40' above street level
(c) 1' x 9' tri-color 12w LED arrray
(d) 10' x 10' 185 watt 24 volt
    photovoltaic panel array at
    60' centers

78

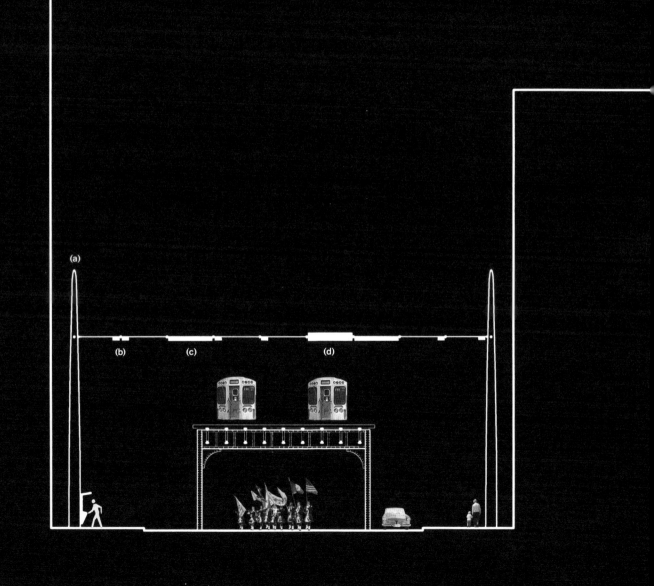

WOODHOUSE

Mine is the educational district.

We're trying to define this as an educational district which we call the "Ed." The loop has the "El" this is the "Ed."

How we're proposing to unify the district is by doing a stainless steel net parallel to the ground and 40 feet up. Called the Ed Net.

TIGERMAN

And how do you support this again structurally?

Structurally we were going to have masts that – you know, the thing is 40 feet off the ground, so I figure that we would go about another 20 feet because you'd have some sort of guide cables that come down and support it. So it just flaps up and down in the wind.

TIGERMAN

Would it have lighting and would it replace the street lighting?

You could replace them. I'd like to do that.

GAROFALO

If you can find a way to control it, control the quality of light – it's all stainless and LED – so it still hangs together. I get worried about advertising.

GANG

I like the word the Ed Net, but I'm not totally convinced the solution is there yet. It seems like it has much more potential, for example, when you see the net you know your getting , like full T-1 activity or something.

Since last time we have concentrated on one thing and that's light. We're thinking of it as a big video screen and each 10 foot square is a pixel.

What we would do then is to have these things programmable because then the entire surface is a programmable video screen in a way.

MARTIN

Would the colors be visible during the day?

Not during the day, and that's the thing we're wrestling with.

TIGERMAN

I really admire your listening to last time's comments and working some of this stuff through. It still has a way to go but it's becoming very sophisticated.

The thing that we were thinking about then on top of it we could put mesh – big mesh panels because you could – you know, you could rig it to have daytime things.

TIGERMAN

What is the diameter of the cable?

I'm thinking maybe three or four inches.

TIGERMAN

And you think structurally it will...

I've talked to lighting people.

I haven't talked to structural people.

TIGERMAN

I would suggest you do.

South Loop
Educational District
David Woodhouse

Mr. Woodhouse received his Bachelor of Architecture degree in 1971 from the University of Illinois in Urbana in a program that included study at the École des Beaux-Arts in Versailles, France. He joined Stanley Tigerman and Associates in 1975. He later joined Booth Hansen Associates in 1980, ultimately becoming a Vice President in the firm, where he honed his talents in cultural and community building design. In 1987, Mr. Woodhouse formed the partnership, Langdon & Woodhouse Architects, and embarked on a series of public and private projects as Principal of his own firm. The practice evolved into David Woodhouse Architects three years later and has remained this entity ever since. The firm's work comprises high-profile assignments for a wide variety of public institutions. The firm has earned both national and local awards from the American Institute of Architects and has been published in numerous periodicals, including *Architectural Record*, *Progressive Architecture* and *Interior Design*. Mr. Woodhouse regularly serves as author, lecturer and educator.

Jeanne Gang
Ohio/Ontario Gateway

Ron Krueck
Northerly Island

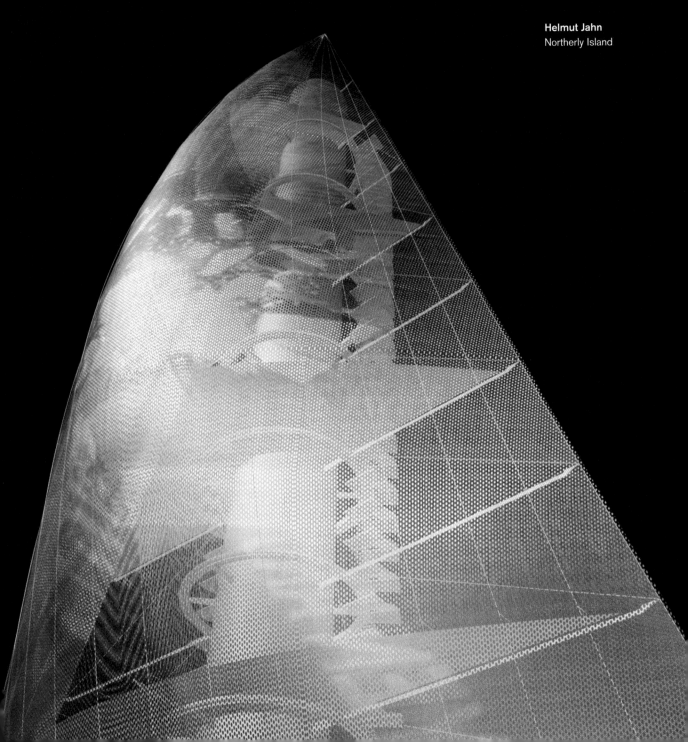

Brad Lynch
Chinatown Gateway

Joe Valerio
The Chicago River

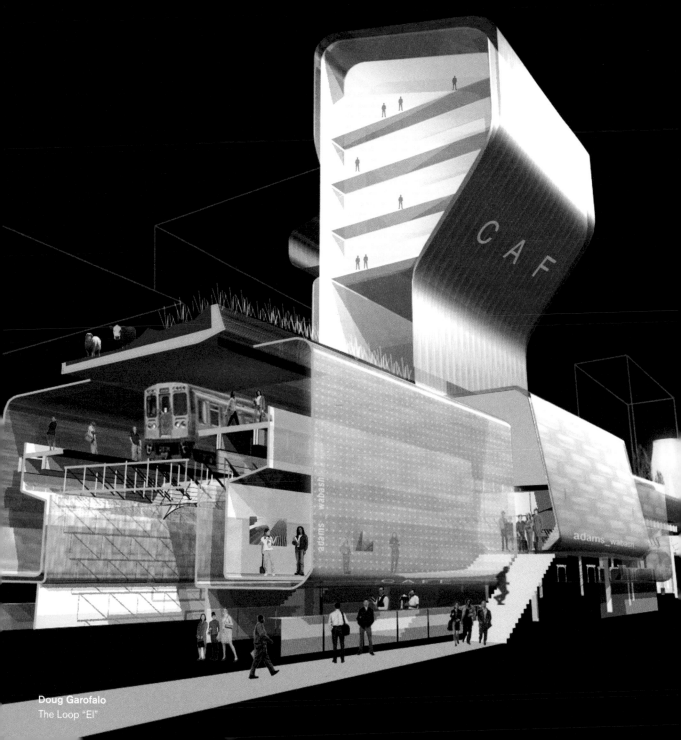

Doug Garofalo
The Loop "El"

John Ronan
The Old Post Office

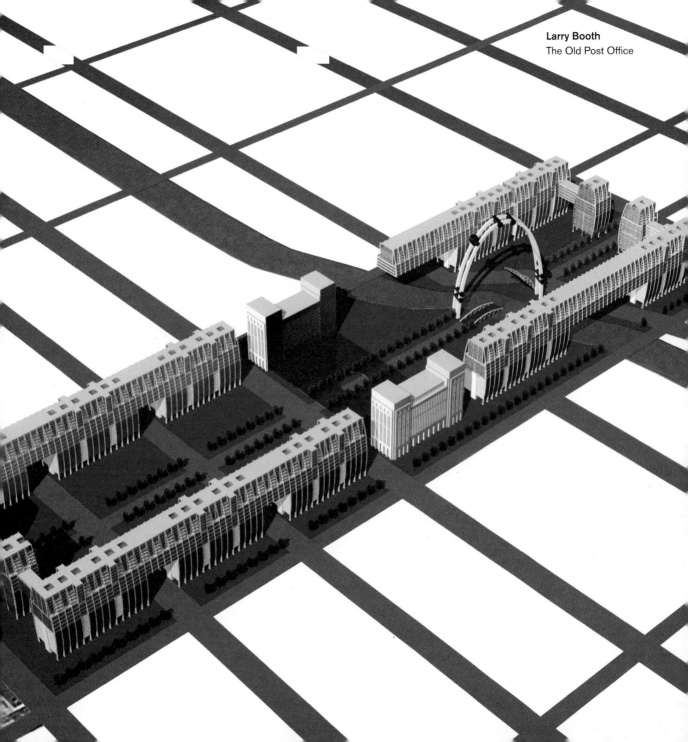

David Woodhouse
South Loop
Educational District

CONTRAST

Ohio/Ontario Gateway
Adrian Smith

Tower C.1

Chicago Gateway Project

The design of a gateway is dependent on the method of travel to and from a place. For the settlers it was often discovered on foot or by boat and later, by train, by car and by airplane. As the mode of transportation evolves, so does the essence of the Gateway. Today due to the variety of ways that cities are engaged, the Gateway is now more virtual than ever. In the future, twenty-five, fifty or perhaps a hundred years from now a Gateway will be defined as a three dimensional point in space; a series of x, y and z coordinates and by a system of navigation that is controlled not by the passenger or driver but by an interactive series of coordinates in space that inform the vehicle of the safest path to its destination and will direct the on board navigator to comply with its directions. These technical innovations, coupled with advances in the structural properties of new materials, not yet conceived, will lead to a new paradigm in our daily lifestyles.

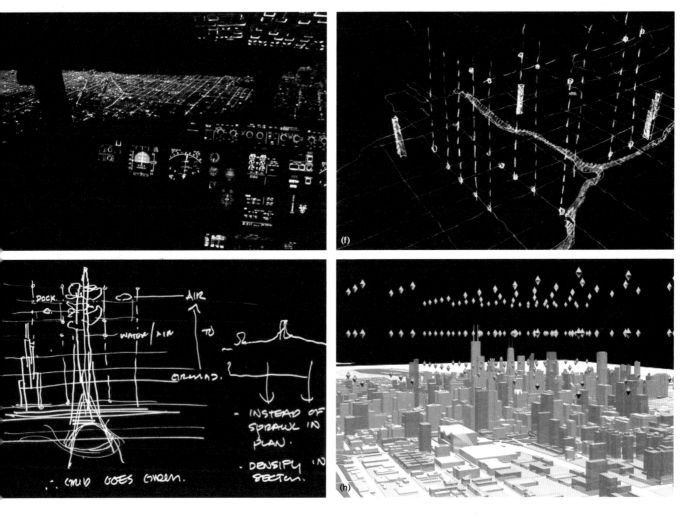

Freed from the constraints of ground transportation and current elevator systems, an advancement of super-tall buildings based on air docks will result and a new form of Gateway will emerge. Old transportation systems will be re-allocated to better public uses such as park space and gardens for leisure activity. This project attempts to conceive what is a prototype gateway piece in a new system of personal travel in the next century.

(a) The Chicago River gateway – 1800's
(b) The Chicago River gateway – 1850's
(c) Chicago Circle Interstate Interchange – 1950's
(d) Current technology in personal air vehicles -
    the Moller M400 Aerocar - VTOL
(e) Gateway as a node in 3-dimensional space,
    an intersection defined by a crossover of systems
(f) Gateway as node in 3-dimensional space
(g) Entering Chicago airspace – the virtual gateway
(h) The gateway as the point of transfer

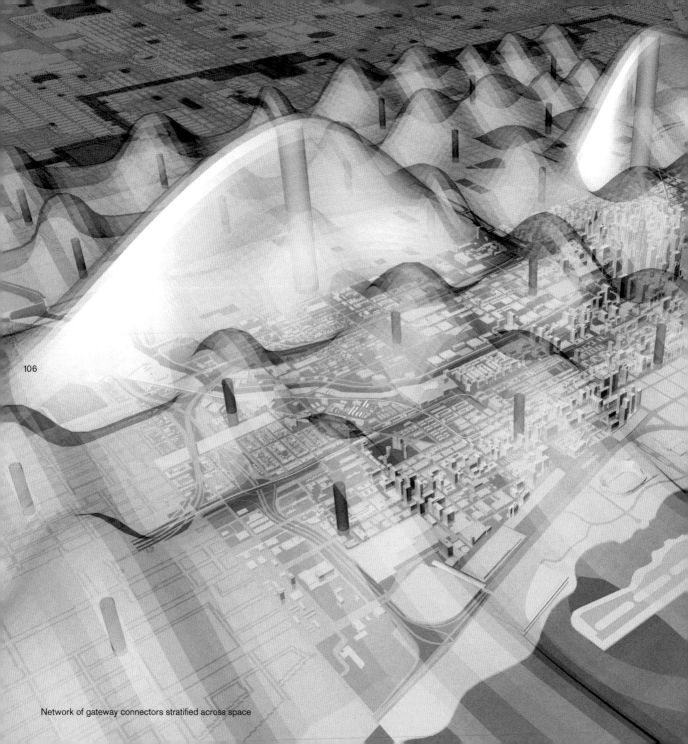

106

Network of gateway connectors stratified across space

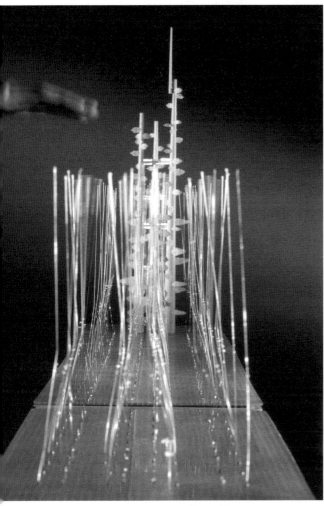

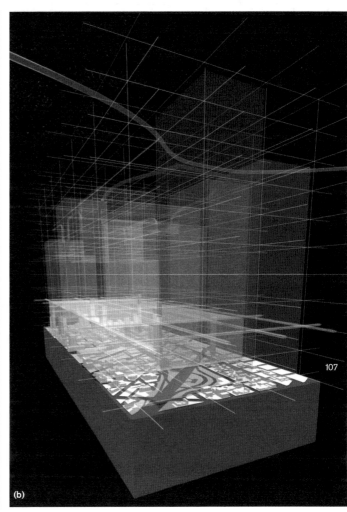

107

A gateway is an ever-changing boundary which adjusts because the city is permeable. A gateway may be defined as a node in 3-dimensional space, and intersection defined by a crossover of systems. The gateway of the future is identified as the point of transfer.

(a) The grid as responsive field
(b) Strata allow gateway access at multiple elevations
(c) As access transitions over time from surface
     to air, the grid goes green

(a) Vertical infrastructure study with neighborhoods,
    skybridge eco-systems and personal air vehicle access
(b) Vertical infrastructure study with access as multiple strata
(c) Vertical infrastructure study with mixed use pods
(d) Infrastructure contains wind turbines, solar collectors
    and eco-systems
(e) Tower infrastructure contains neighborhoods
    and points of air vehicle access

(a)

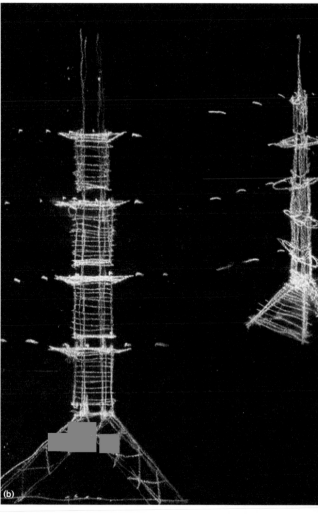

(b)

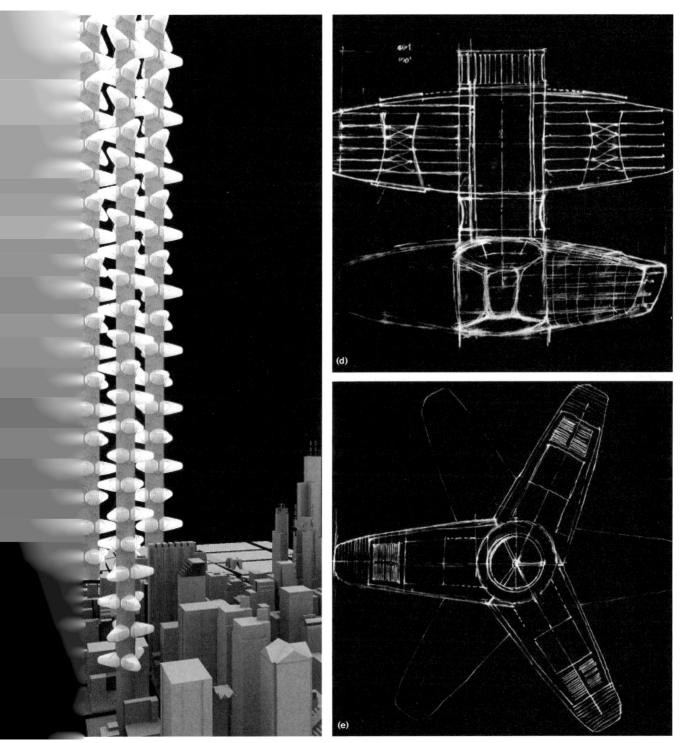

(d)

(e)

(a) The Ohio Street axis

(b) Vertical infrastructure: neighborhoods,
   skybridge eco-systems

(c) The future as envisioned in the past – 1930's

(d) An architectural response to the point
   of transfer – 1930's

(e) Science fiction vision of the future

(d)

SMITH

When I started looking at the Ohio/Ontario corridor, slash gateway, I started out looking at it very – from a very minute perspective.

So I started asking questions, what is a gateway; a threshold, portal, symbol, entry and transition?

Gateways a hundred years ago were different than gateways today for the City of Chicago, and where are they going to be 100 years from now?

In the future I think the gateway can be defined as a vertical system as well as a horizontal system – creating zones in the sky that are for different kinds of travel.

TIGERMAN

Is this like an amalgam of what both Solari talked about – and actually Bruce?

I don't think he got into a what-if mode of transportation.

TIGERMAN

No. But it was an interesting observation.

I'm just saying 100 years ago, maybe 125 years ago, the automobile wasn't invented. Look how it changed our world.

ROSS BARNEY

What happened at the ground plane?
What do you imagine the ground plane to be?

Well, I thought the ground plane for the most part could become more leisure-oriented for people to recreate and to have gardens and –

ROSS BARNEY

What about private ownership of land?

BEEBY

That would be the question; are people willing to give up the notion of ownership of a piece of land and the emotional attachment?

JOHNSON

Well, they don't own the roads now.
Why not keep the road as public domain?

BEEBY

It's a question of human nature. I mean, its kind of people are so grounded in the idea of land.

I don't think so anymore. People are very comfortable buying a unit in the air.

BEEBY

Does that redevelop or does that actually go back into a pool, because Bucky Fuller had this idea of floating spheres, and the world turns back to wilderness.

For a period of time you'd be in a transition. But, you know, we're now greening railroads into greenways now.

Ohio/Ontario Gateway
Adrian Smith

Adrian D. Smith is a Consulting Design Partner in the Chicago office of Skidmore, Owings & Merrill LLP. Since joining SOM in 1967, his work has shown an evolving interest in the use of the vernacular and classical forms and compositions together with state-of-the-art systems and technologies to integrate new buildings into the adjacent fabric. In all his designs, Mr. Smith stresses contextualism to achieve urban continuity. His designs are sensitive to the projects' physical environment, taking into consideration conditions such as location, climate, cultural and social influences in order to achieve cultural and environmental sustainability. During his tenure as Design Partner, projects under Mr. Smith's leadership and direction have received over 90 architecture, engineering, planning and interior design awards including six international awards, six National AIA awards. 23 Chicago Chapter AIA awards and 11 energy awards.

with
Gordon Gill
Alex Martinez
Les Ventsch

photography
Steinkamp Ballog

Northerly Island
Helmut Jahn

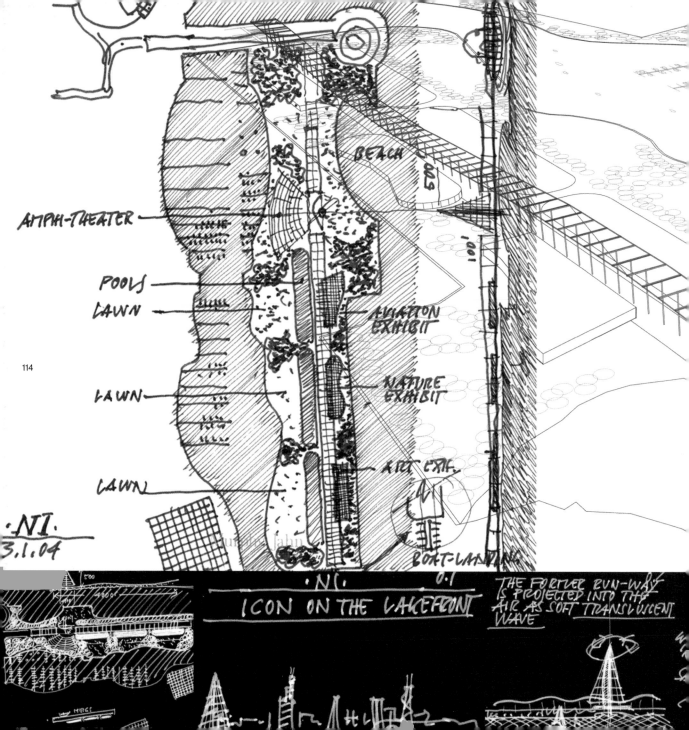

AMPH-THEATER

POOLS

LAWN

LAWN

LAWN

BEACH

AVIATION EXHIBIT

NATURE EXHIBIT

ART EXH.

BOAT-LANDING

114

·NI·
3.1.04

·NI·
ICON ON THE LAKEFRONT

THE FORMER RUN-WAY IS PROJECTED INTO THE AIR AS SOFT TRANSLUCENT WAVE

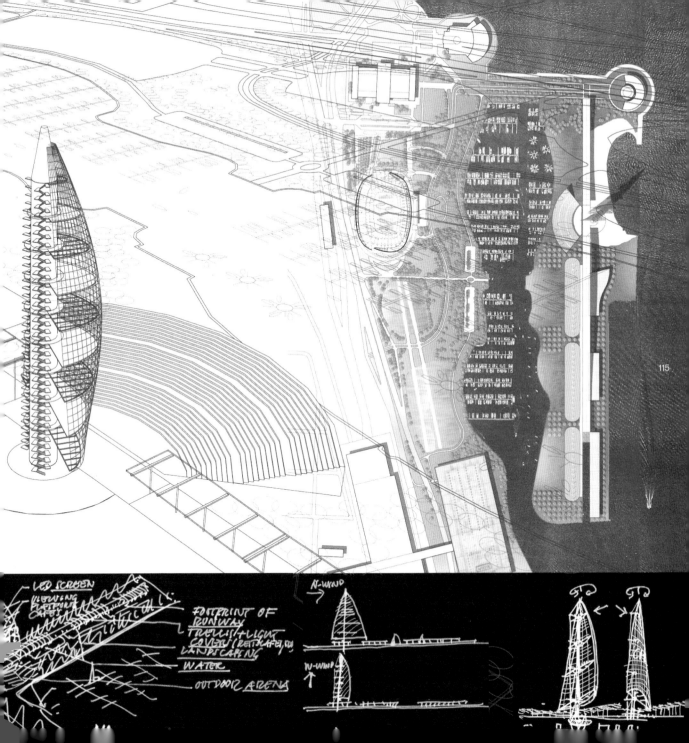

VED SCREEN
VIEWING
PLATFORM
CAFES

FOOTPRINT OF
RUNWAY
TRELLIS/LIGHT
COVER (RETBRACES) ON
LANDSCAPING
WATER
OUTDOOR ARENA

N-WIND

W-WIND

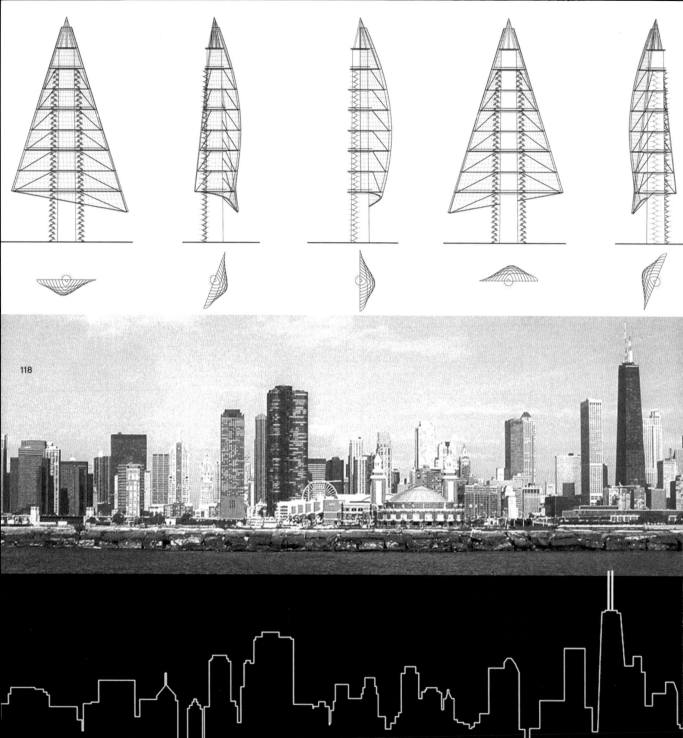

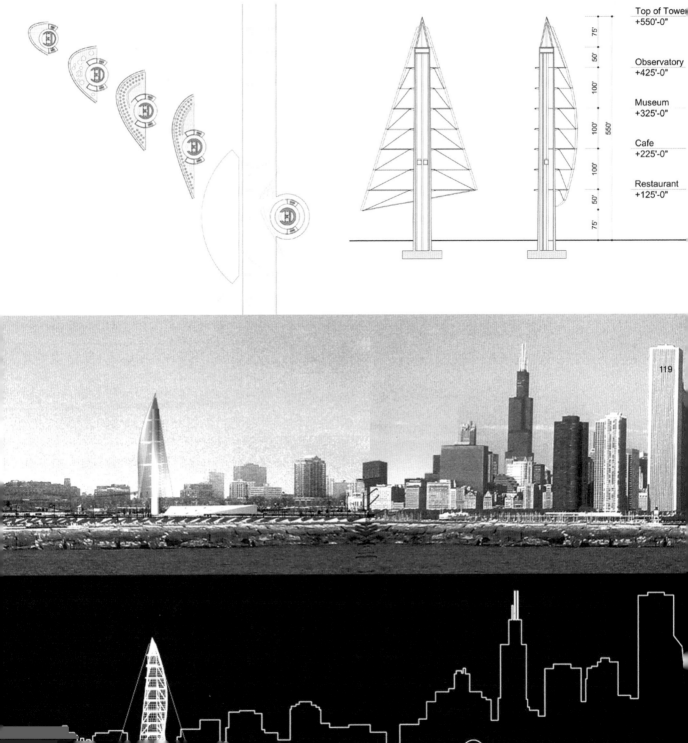

Top of Tower
+550'-0"

Observatory
+425'-0"

Museum
+325'-0"

Cafe
+225'-0"

Restaurant
+125'-0"

75'
50'
100'
100'
100'
50'
75'

550'

119

500'

100'

Sailtower

Northerly Island was for many years known as Meigs Field, a small airport for limited commercial and private service, occupying the peninsula at Chicago's lakefront. Flying in and out of it, one could experience magnificent views of Chicago's skyline and lakefront. It was simply exhilarating and breathtaking.

This proposal for a Lakefront Park in its place proposes an iconic 550' Sailtower to mark the horizontality of this place on the lakefront, which allows visitors to experience on its various levels the same excitement.

Close to it are McCormick Place and Soldier Field, two structures that are built on the remnants of their original configurations, leading to controversial but unique results.

We adopted this tie to the archeology of a place as generator for the plan of the park. The former runway becomes the axis for access from land and water and the organizing spine for placing the Tower with an Amphitheater, various Museums, Restaurants and Cafes. At the former taxiways, connections occur to the natural landscape and the great lawns, which are used for play and entertainment. A light roof, floating like a wave, protects the activities below it.

The wind turns the Sailtower into different positions, which gives it a constantly changing reading, based on the natural conditions. Its platforms, accessible by stairs and elevators, house Restaurants, Cafes, Museums and places for viewing and entertainment. The Tower becomes a vertical extension of the Park.

The Sail of the Tower is a medialized, transparent LED-screen. Its software will allow it to be used for message, information and representation of art and products in a controlled and sophisticated way. It is not meant for advertising or videos, but a new way how the City, the State, Tourism, Business and Industry present themselves at this place. The ephemeral nature of the Tower creates an ever-changing perception during day and night. The mast, boom and rigging together with the stairs, elevators and platforms become a visible diagram of the different layers and multiple functions.

The Amphitheater becomes an important counterpoint to the Tower who can be either background or the object on stage, performing with its movement and medialization continuously to an assembled audience.

Such a structure requires state of the art engineering, construction and materials. Next to more conventional materials, like concrete, steel and glass, new materials like carbon fibers and plastics are used to achieve ultimate lightweight construction and maximum performance.

Like nature facilitates its movements, so does it make the Tower energy efficient and sustainable. Wind turbines, integral piping and rainwater collection use the natural resources of wind, sun, water and convert it to electricity, heat or allows its reuse.

The Sailtower makes a statement as an urban icon on the lakefront. It marks a new park, which otherwise would not be seen. It is dynamic and mobile and elevates construction to a level of art.

JAHN

Can I go next? I didn't know this meeting would last this long - I have a presentation to go to.

TIGERMAN

Helmut has Northerly Island - Go Helmut.

I felt whatever is done on Northerly Island should reflect what the plan was before. There's something nice about an airport, its a great image.

I felt there needed to be a vertical icon, something which marks the place as being not an airport anymore, but being a park and being something where people go.

So the idea is to have, over the former runway, a floating roof - somehow floats and has no columns. And then there's a tower, a sail tower which actually moves with the wind, so as the wind comes from different directions, the image of the building would change. And so on the skyline you have this 500-600 foot tower - the sail tower becomes a vertical extension of the activities on the ground.

TIGERMAN

So it actually is the park that the Mayor wants to do but in a totally different way. It's very cool. Can I make a suggestion? The first thing I thought of —and don't take umbrage of it. I think about a shopping center, you know, which has destination points at each end. But what makes one go to the end and back again and again?

Somehow it was kind of intuitive. I don't think you're going to see a lot of new stuff actually.

TIGERMAN

I figured because you had so developed it the last time.

So the idea is to do that tower which is about 550'. Horizontal places in history, you know, have been marked by a vertical element, whether its churches and towers and city halls, whether it's in Venice or Sienna. The old runway alignment becomes an organizing element for placement of the tower and amphitheater and the former taxiways they become connections with a more natural landscape and some great lawns used for play. A very light roof covers the runway, like a wave, association obviously to the water and protects the activities below it.

TIGERMAN

Actually, I think for me personally, the most interesting part of the scheme is not the tower, it's the memory of the runway and using it as an organizing element.

ROSS BARNEY

I like the Tower but I also wonder why it's sited where it is.

Because that's where I decided it was going to be.

Northerly Island
Helmut Jahn

Born in Germany, Jahn graduated from the Technische Hochschule in Munich. He came to the United States for graduate studies in architecture at the Illinois Institute of Technology. After attending IIT, he went to work at C. F. Murphy Assoc. where he worked as Project Architect under Gene Summers, designing the new McCormick Place. In 1976, his first major high-rise building in Chicago, Xerox Centre, won great critical acclaim.
Today, as President and Chief Executive Officer of Murphy/ Jahn, he has been called Chicago's premiere architect who has dramatically changed the face of Chicago. His growing national and international reputation has led to commissions across the United States, Europe, Africa and Asia. He is committed to design excellence and the improvement of the urban environment. His projects have been recognized globally for design innovation, vitality and integrity. From the numerous publications on his work, one understands the excitement his work has generated in the public eye as well as professional journals and press.

with
Francisco Gonzalez-Pulido

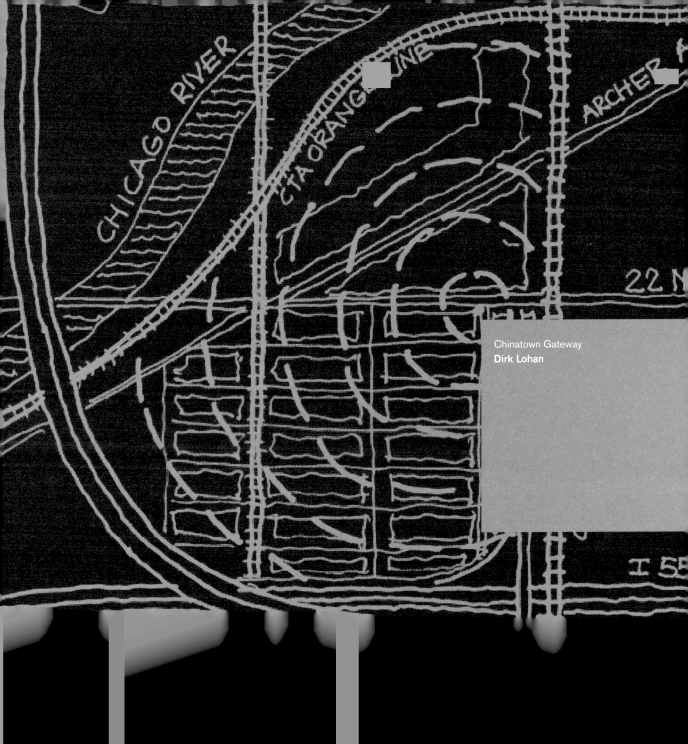

CHICAGO RIVER

CTA ORANGE LINE

ARCHER A

22 N

Chinatown Gateway
Dirk Lohan

I 55

Background

Chinatown, near Cermak Road and Wentworth Avenue, is a stable neighborhood that exhibits a recognizable identity which is uniquely its own. Throughout the 100 years of its existence, Chinatown sustained a largely segregated existence with little connection to other neighborhoods because of a complete encirclement on all sides by major road structures, multiple railroad lines, CTA elevated tracks and the Chicago River. This virtual isolation is the major reason for the unspoiled Chinese character of the neighborhood but it is also an anachronism in America where people are increasingly connected and integrated.

An Iconic Symbol

To overcome the isolation of this hidden enclave the idea loomed large to create an iconic symbol that would render Chinatown visible and instantly recognizable in the skyline of Chicago. The ubiquitous existence of the "Dragon Tower" as a symbol of hope and good luck in Chinese art and history emerged as the appropriate architectural image that could achieve a heightened recognition of Chinatown's existence.

Robotic Parking

A tall cylindrical parking tower is envisioned to accommodate up to 4200 of tourist and convention visitor vehicles, thus alleviating the parking burden in both downtown and around McCormick Place. To handle such quantities efficiently, the tower will be operated exclusively by a robotic parking system, which functions like a warehouse storage and retrieval mechanism. The passengers would never have to enter the tower beyond the ground-level drop-off and exit bays, except to go to the observatory at the top from which breathtaking views in all directions can be enjoyed.

From the location of the Dragon Tower one would directly access the Interstate system as well as walk to the CTA stations with direct connections to the Loop, the South side and Midway airport. Additionally, it is proposed that the Chicago River be widened into a boat basin that reaches the foot of the tower. From here one might take sightseeing boats through the city all the way to Michigan Avenue and Navy Pier.

Dragon Tower

114 levels of parking platforms
36 cars per level
4,104 car capacity
1,054 feet tall

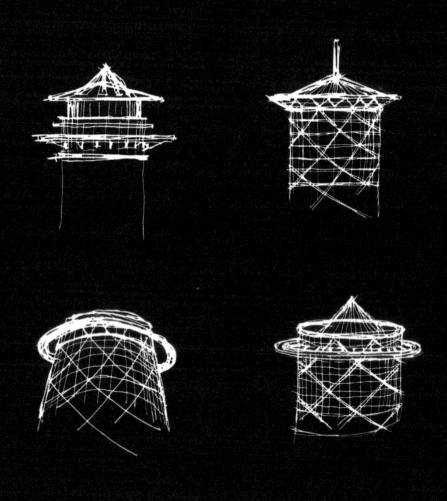

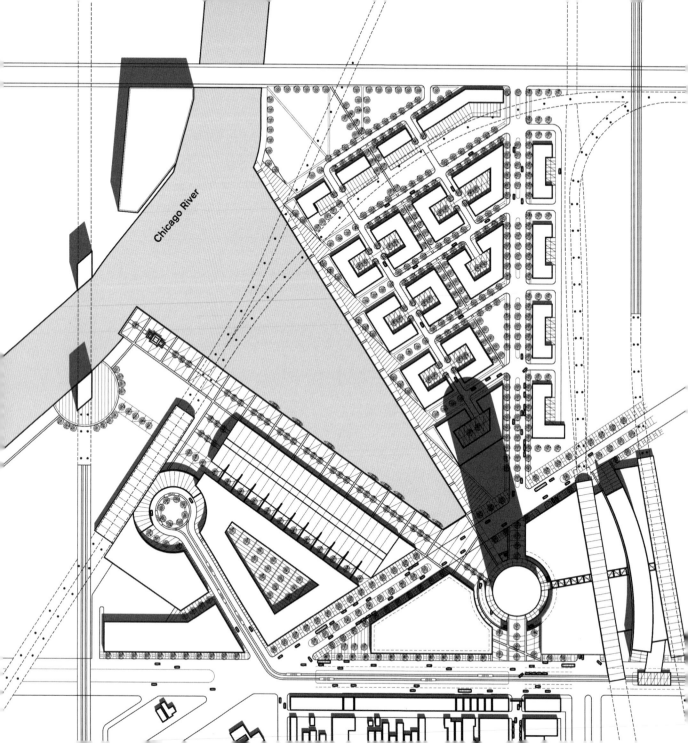

Chicago River

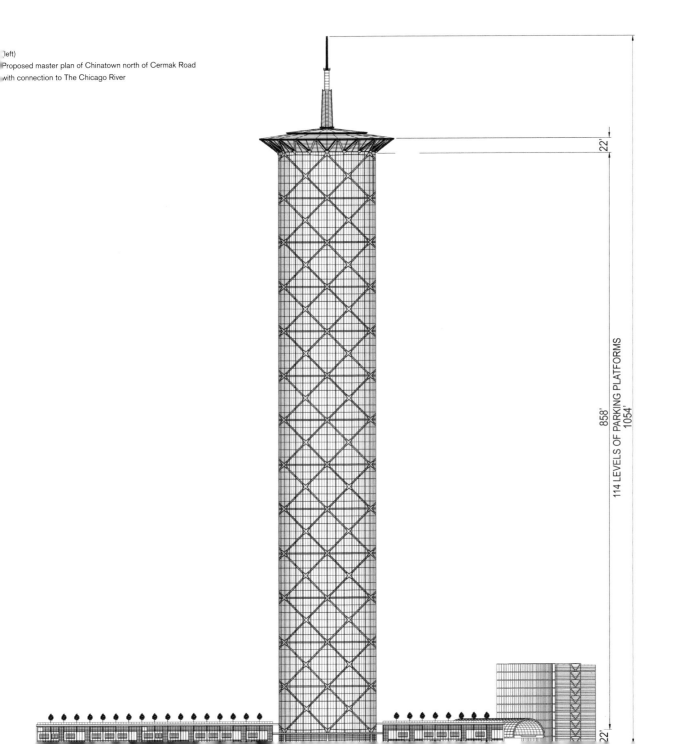

(left)
Proposed master plan of Chinatown north of Cermak Road
with connection to The Chicago River

22'

114 LEVELS OF PARKING PLATFORMS
1054'

858'

22'

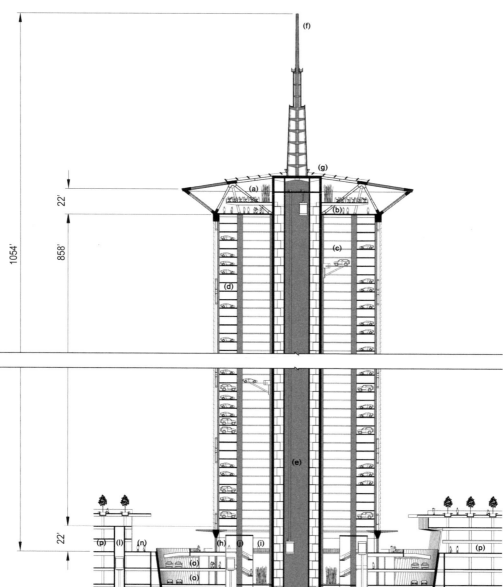

(left)
(a) Restaurant
(b) Observation lounge
(c) Robotic lift arm
(d) Vehicle platform
(e) Express elevator core
(f) Communication mast
(g) Rooftop skylights
(h) Lobby
(i) Lobby/core bridge
(j) Glass enclosed elevator/stairs
(k) Service corridor
(l) Freight elevator
(m) Roof garden
(n) Wharf plaza
(o) Vehicular circulation ring
(p) Retail building

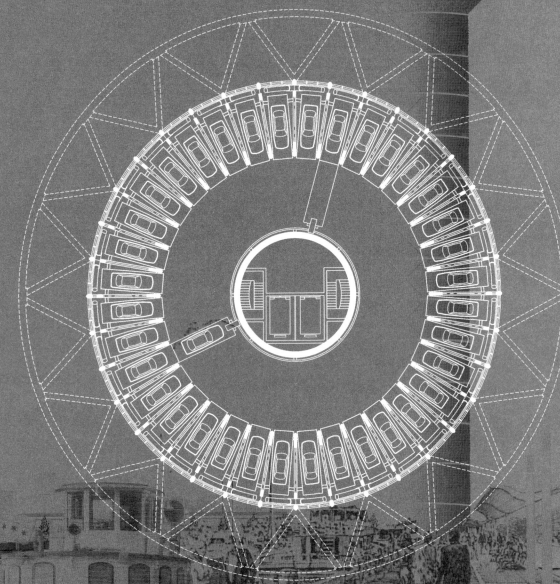

(top)
Typical floor plan showing parked cars

(bottom)
View of the Dragon Tower as seen from the proposed Chinatown Wharf

130

View North on Wentworth Avenue

LOHAN

One of the things that's kicking around in my head, Stanley, is really an old idea that I drew up once, in fact at the Central Area Committee. I would like to revisit that and make Chinatown the impetus for the turning point of extending the Chicago River and connect it back to the Lake.

TIGERMAN

Yeah. I think it's a great idea that should be revisited.

As part of it I would like to do some special feature in Chinatown to make it notable.

JAHN

It's funny how you don't forget those things. I remember that.

Part of the idea would be to move the existing locks to the outer breakwater and extend the whole breakwater and make the breakwater an enclosure so the whole lakefront in front of Downtown becomes a lagoon.

SMITH

That's a great idea.

As you know I said that I was going to continue or redevelop an earlier idea of extending the Chicago River to the Lake near Chinatown. Upon reflection of that idea, I canned it.

Chinatown, like no other place in Chicago is really enclosed and closed to the outer world. So one of the concerns that I think – or one of the issues that I felt is that Chinatown needs to be made noticeable and recognizable as a presence in the city. As I walked around Chinatown I noticed these unusual towers they had erected at the north and south end of Wentworth. I happen to know a little bit about Chinese art and history, primarily because my name is actually Chinese. There are 18 Lohans in Chinese mythology. So anyway, these towers are called dragon towers. So the idea was to build a tower, and as I talked to the people and merchants they feel very constrained and parking is a big issue.

BEEBY

How tall is it?

1,054 feet with an observation deck on top.

JAHN

Who would like his car a thousand feet in the air?

If you were driving in from Indiana on the Dan Ryan you would see this tower.

Chinatown Gateway
Dirk Lohan

Dirk Lohan is a founder of Lohan Anderson, and is responsible for the firm's designs and long-term development. Lohan left his native Germany to begin his architectural studies at the Illinois Institute of Technology under the tutelage of his grandfather, Mies van der Rohe. He returned to Germany and finished his studies in architecture and planning at the Technische Hochschule (Diplom-Ingenieur), Munich in 1962. When Mr. Lohan returned to Chicago, he worked closely with Mies on such projects as the New National Gallery in Berlin, the IBM office building in Chicago and The Toronto Dominion Centre. Prior to the establishment of Lohan Anderson, Mr. Lohan was the senior principal in the predecessor firms of: Lohan Associates (1986-2002) and Lohan Caprile Goettsch (2002-2004). Under his leadership, the firm produced an impressive portfolio of design solutions including such projects as the McDonald's Corporate Headquarters Campus, the John G. Shedd Oceanarium, and the Sinai Temple as well as national and international projects.

with
Christopher Hurst
Anthony Kempa

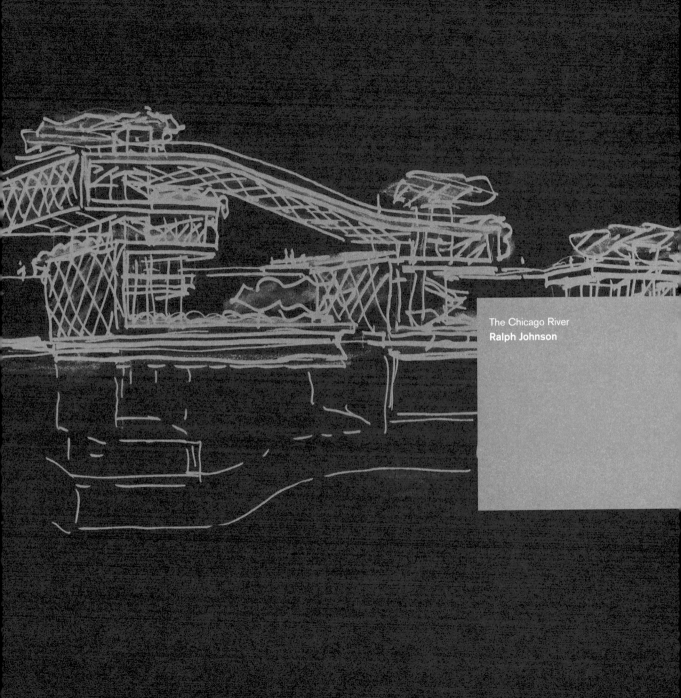

The Chicago River
Ralph Johnson

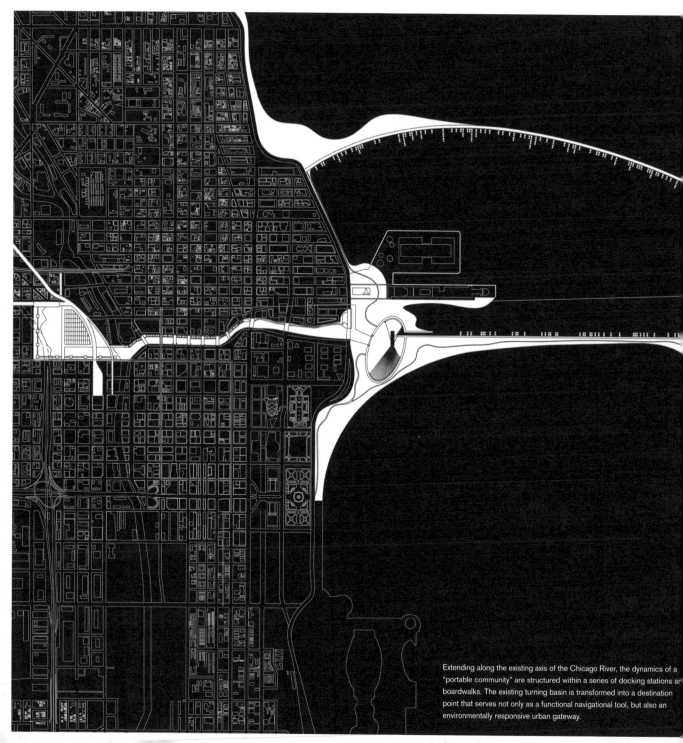

Extending along the existing axis of the Chicago River, the dynamics of a "portable community" are structured within a series of docking stations and boardwalks. The existing turning basin is transformed into a destination point that serves not only as a functional navigational tool, but also an environmentally responsive urban gateway.

(left)

Kinzie Station

The existing train lines located west of the fork in the Chicago River are currently disruptive to development of the area. Consolidating these lines and channeling the river westward generates an urban lagoon that could become home to a new typology of building, constructed of reused materials, and a reinvigorated community adapted to a culture it potentially displaces.

(middle)

Chicago River

A majority of the existing riverwalk is inconsistent, interrupted and thus underutilized. A "flotilla" of salvaged barges that hold public events, retail, restaurants and parks could create a continuous experience along the river as well as provide destination points that would activate the area year-round.

(right)

River Lock

The mouth of the Chicago River is instrumental to Chicago's boat enthusiast culture and tourist industry. Its function no longer serves as the critical gateway for industry, but as a roadblock to pedestrians and lakefront continuity. By preserving the structure and function of the lock and adding a reorganized turning basin, a revitalized iconography of the river and lakefront can be established.

135

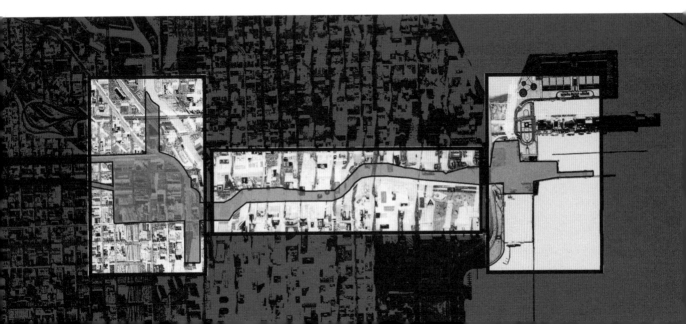

(above)
The existing tracks at the fork of the river define an inner zone of land that
is extremely unviable and disturbed by this condition. These tracks currently
converge a couple miles west of the river. The scheme consolidates the two
parallel running lines under a multi-level park berm. The regained interior
space receives an extended channel of the river to form an urban lagoon
surrounded by a development of point towers for Chicago's homeless community and a plot of land containing a variety of mixed use developments.
The bermed over train tracks establishes a new opportunity for pedestrian
movement along a currently underutilized artery throughout the city.

(right)
Homeless living under the existing train lines with collected furnishings
and possessions

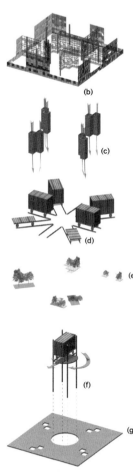

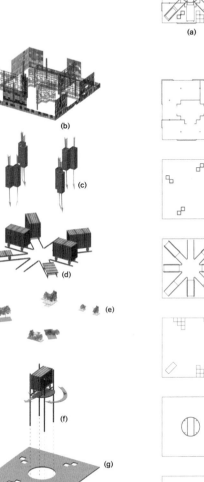

(right)

The homeless towers provide an environment that accommodates the needs of portability, shelter, and community. Reused and recycled materials form a modular framework that can be continuously adjusted. Modified train cars can be "checked out" at a central hub and transported to various spaces within the towers.

(a) Typical Level Plan
(b) Reused Scaffolding and Recycled Cardboard Wall Panels
(c) Service Tubes

(d) Train Cart Units
(e) Garden Modules
(f) Revolving Cart Hoist
(g) Floor Plate

(below)

Flotillas of recycled barges line the north side of the river, starting from the east branch. A continuous walkway stretches the entire length providing an uninterrupted pedestrian experience along the river.

The flotillas are movable platforms that can be relocated along the river. A hydraulic "core" allows floor plates and an elastometric skin to collapse and expand for transport under the bridges. This provides and autonomy of relocation without the regimented scheduling of bridge openings.

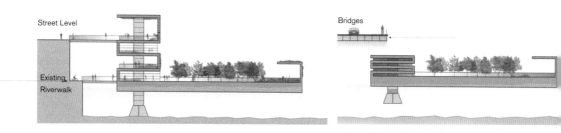

Street Level

Existing Riverwalk

Bridges

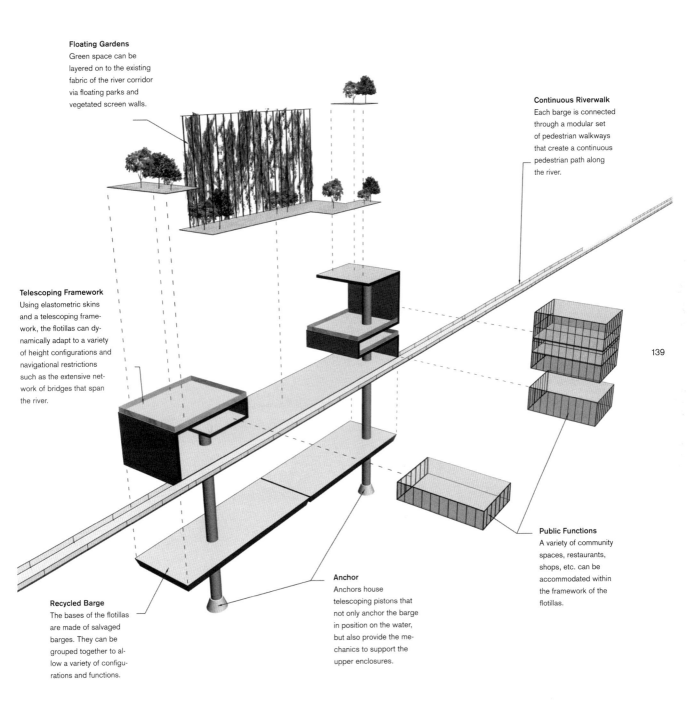

Floating Gardens
Green space can be layered on to the existing fabric of the river corridor via floating parks and vegetated screen walls.

Continuous Riverwalk
Each barge is connected through a modular set of pedestrian walkways that create a continuous pedestrian path along the river.

Telescoping Framework
Using elastometric skins and a telescoping framework, the flotillas can dynamically adapt to a variety of height configurations and navigational restrictions such as the extensive network of bridges that span the river.

139

Public Functions
A variety of community spaces, restaurants, shops, etc. can be accommodated within the framework of the flotillas.

Recycled Barge
The bases of the flotillas are made of salvaged barges. They can be grouped together to allow a variety of configurations and functions.

Anchor
Anchors house telescoping pistons that not only anchor the barge in position on the water, but also provide the mechanics to support the upper enclosures.

Historically, the Chicago River has been instrumental in transforming Chicago into the metropolis it is today. It was an existing natural element that was a gateway to settlers and ultimately a passage through the inner workings of a modern city. Over time, the impacts of railroads, interstates, and air travel diminished the demand of the city's requirements for the purely functional aspects of the main branch of the river. It evolved into more of a casual passageway to the lake for the general public and a destination spot for tourists. By coding certain aspects of its past and present conditions and applying contemporary concepts of reusable/renewable resources this proposal looks to reorganize the contemporary forces that define the character of the river. Establishing a framework not only reinvigorates functional opportunities but celebrates its importance within the image of the city.

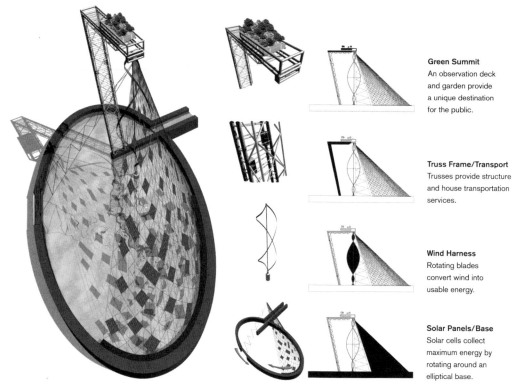

Green Summit
An observation deck and garden provide a unique destination for the public.

Truss Frame/Transport
Trusses provide structure and house transportation services.

Wind Harness
Rotating blades convert wind into usable energy.

Solar Panels/Base
Solar cells collect maximum energy by rotating around an elliptical base.

(right)
View looking east toward the turning basin

(above)
The proposed turning basin becomes a sculptural gateway element for the city. It provides both an expanded network of parkland and beaches and a pedestrian bridge that rotates along the perimeter of the basin to allow boat access and renewable energy elements, such as a photovoltaic solar net and a Darrieus wind turbine.

TIGERMAN
Ralph do you want to do the River next?

You don't have to use computers, right?

JOHNSON
No. I did sketches.

TIGERMAN
Cool. Just like the old days.

BEEBY
Ralph used to work for Stanley.

You're the only one that actually lived through that.

You know how to respond.

I kind of thought about the River as it is right now. But it seems like the one thing that's missing was kind of a life to the spaces that are being created out of nothing. So I had this idea to float barges, barges that you can float in and that could actually have structures on them which could activate the riverfront.

TIGERMAN
So while I think this is visionary –

I think it has a sense of believability.

I don't know what the rules are, but I might be breaking them.

TIGERMAN
Screw them. I mean, this is a visionary scheme.

ROSS BARNEY
I think I should tell you this, that we have this project with the City. I could give you what I know.

I don't know if I want to know.

Based on a conversation I had with Carol after the last meeting and we had lunch just last week, I rethought the barge idea, and where it should be, and I flipped it to the other side of the river, which works a lot better.

Then I wanted to broaden the scope of the whole thing. So it's three-part now. The barges, dealing with the locks and making some kind of gateway, and working on the area where the river splits at the west end. We went through the site on the west end and found homeless people camped out underneath the viaducts. So we had the idea of making it like homeless point towers with kind of a warming station at the end.

BEEBY
The only thing I'm worried about is the kind of social housing and the SRO cardboard boxes is a little tough, don't you think?

It's some part of history of the site though. We thought it was – we kind of found the site and found people living there. So we didn't want to displace them. The whole idea evolves around found objects, either found barges or found spaces.

TIGERMAN
The only thing you haven't done is the American bridge from U.S. Steel to Indiana.

We're working on it.

The Chicago River
Ralph Johnson

Ralph E. Johnson, received his Bachelor of Architecture from the University of Illinois and his Master of Architecture from Harvard University. He began his career at Stanley Tigerman's office and then joined Perkins & Will in 1976, where he currently serves as its National Design Director and is a member of its Board of Directors. His projects have been honored with more than 40 design awards, including seven national Honor Awards and numerous regional Honor Awards from the American Institute of Architects and a Progressive Architecture Design Award. He was elected to College of Fellows of the American Institute of Architects in 1995. His work has been published in *Architecture*, *Architectural Record*, *Domus*, *Architecture and Urbanisum* and *L'Architecture D'Aujourd'hui* and other international journals. Monographs on his works were published by Rizzoli in 1995, and by L'Arca in 1998. His work has been exhibited at the Art Institute of Chicago, the Paris Biennale, the Architecture League of New York, the National Building Museum and the Sao Paolo Biennale.

with
Todd Snapp
Adam Freise

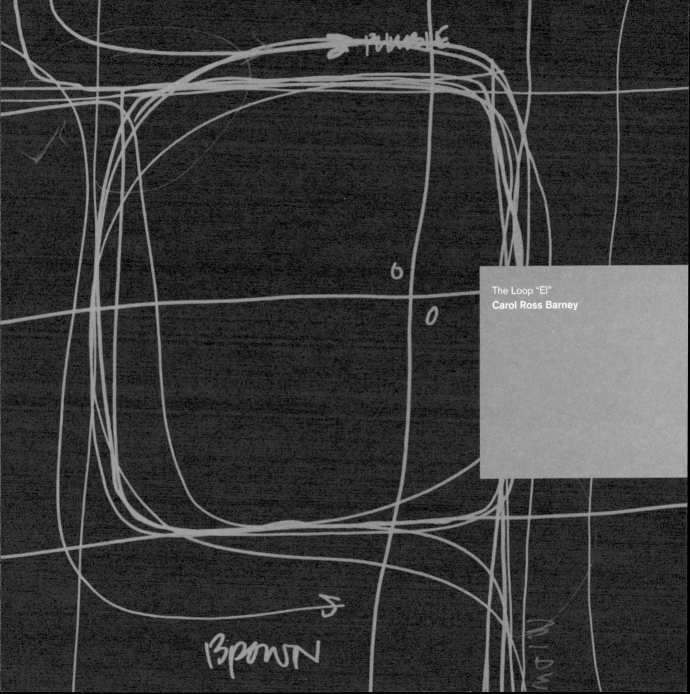

The Loop "El"
Carol Ross Barney

Hortus Urbi

garden (reclaimed)
in the city

In 1909, Daniel Burnham and Edward Bennett published the landmark Plan of Chicago. The most important systems were transportation and parks. Chicago's motto is *urbs in horto*, city in a garden. In 2002, Chicago ranked 11th out of the 12 high density American city with 8.1% park land as percent of city land area. Despite this low ranking, Chicago has the opportunity to add parkland to its urban core by refurbishing the public right of way under the loop elevated tracks as a new type of urban park.

Open the ROW

Vacate ROW under the tracks: Wabash, Van Buren, Wells and Lake for pedestrian use only. Cross streets remain active. Relocate CTA Stations into adjacent buildings. Replace platforms with new translucent platforms. Remove platform canopies. Construct retractable, photovoltaic shades supported from existing buildings at platforms. Allow private development of airspace for recreation and retail.

The "El" as Datum

Strip and paint historic structure red creating park identity and way finding baseline. Build steam and water ponds at Wells/Lake and Wabash/Van Buren for visual and sensory train gateways.

Transit Trees

Construct and plant transit tube: clean air, reduce noise, and produce shade.

Gardens for the People

Obtain underutilized parcels for organic growth of park into adjacent blocks and linkage to parks and plazas. Create civic space to contain public events. Create multiple natural textured gardens for casual vegetal encounters by shoppers and workers.

Destination

Chicago visitors and citizens use mass transit and experience unique garden environment in commercial center.

(right)
Plan landscaped gardens in framework of loop elevated structure under Wells; Wells Street pedestrian pathways in greened ROW

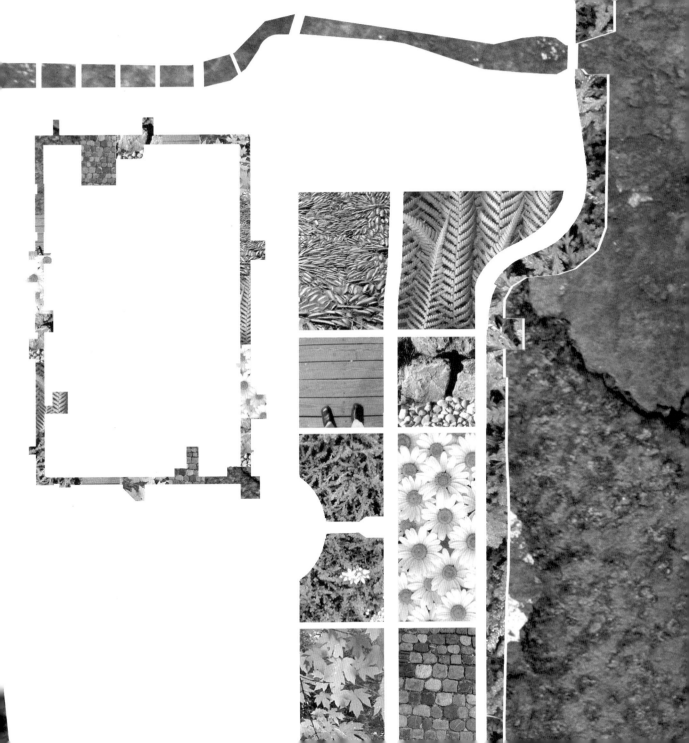

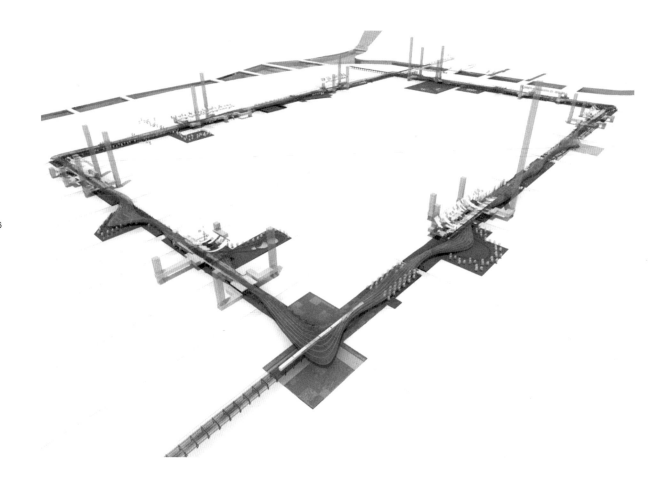

(above)
Wabash multi-layered transit commercial garden

(right)
Wabash birds' eye

(a)

(a) Wells Street pedestrian pathways
in greened ROW
(b) Wabash Street commercial enhanced
by vegetal textures
(c) Adams/Wabash transitional gateway
unites commercial to cultural
(d) green growth new garden on
under utilized urban land
(e) Adams/Wabash transparent
photovoltaic canopy and platform

(c)

(e)

(above)
urban textures rock garden
under transit trees

(right)
in the green tube passengers
experience park landscape

ROSS BARNEY

You know, I have this on my computer, but I also have it on paper.

TIGERMAN

Us old guys are more comfortable looking at paper.

I have the Loop elevated. What's really hard about this problem its about sidewalks, commercial districts, transit and retail. Quite frankly I have trouble figuring out what piece I need to address. We have to call it an overhaul. We looked at some crazy ideas and not so crazy ideas, about the space.

We proposed rather than building a new station we would suspend a roof from building to building, or to please the Mayor you'd make a solar fabric and then you power the "El" from this.

TIGERMAN

Bucky Fuller again.

You could also enclose it to protect people from the effect of it, turn it into a tree, you know, Mayor Daley's greening of the Loop, you could plant all around it, and this concept puts turbines in it so you can actually power the loop from the loop.

TIGERMAN

What's interesting is your study of what's inside, outside, turbine, that stores are the stations, so forth is the kind of research that ought to transpire on a project like this.

Last time I sort of showed a catalog of ideas, and now I'm concentrating on a few pieces that I think could realistically be accomplished. I kind of reverted to what the assignment was, which was the environment underneath the "El".

We took station enclosure and we raised it up seven or eight stories and expanded it from building to building. What we've done is turn Wabash into a giant terminal. We also plan to make this space vibrant by doing walkways and retail space actually over the "El". And you can sort of see we have little glass bridges. So it's a future organic approach to growing a second floor retail.

Finally, we've grown the tube. Year one would start out with very few plantings, but it would grow until it becomes a park in the street.

BEEBY

You never altered the existing structure?

I think we will alter it. It's still a train traveling 14-16 ft above the street.

The Loop 'El'
Carol Ross Barney

Carol Ross Barney is founder and President of Ross Barney + Jankowski. Ross Barney is a graduate of the University of Illinois at Urbana Champaign. Following graduation, she served as a U.S. Peace Corps volunteer in Costa Rica planning national parks. She has taught at the University of Illinois at Chicago, the University of Oklahoma (Goff Chair for Creative Architecture) and the Illinois Institute of Technology where she serves on the College Board of Overseers. Her drawings have been widely exhibited and collected by the Art Institute of Chicago, the Chicago Historical Society, The Museum of Contemporary Art Chicago and the National Building Museum.
Recent commissions include the new United States Federal Building in Oklahoma City, the United States Border Station in Sault Ste. Marie Michigan, a new laboratory building for the University of Minnesota at Duluth and reconstruction of two of Chicago's most heavily used transit stations at Fullerton and Belmont Avenues.

with
Daniel Pohrte

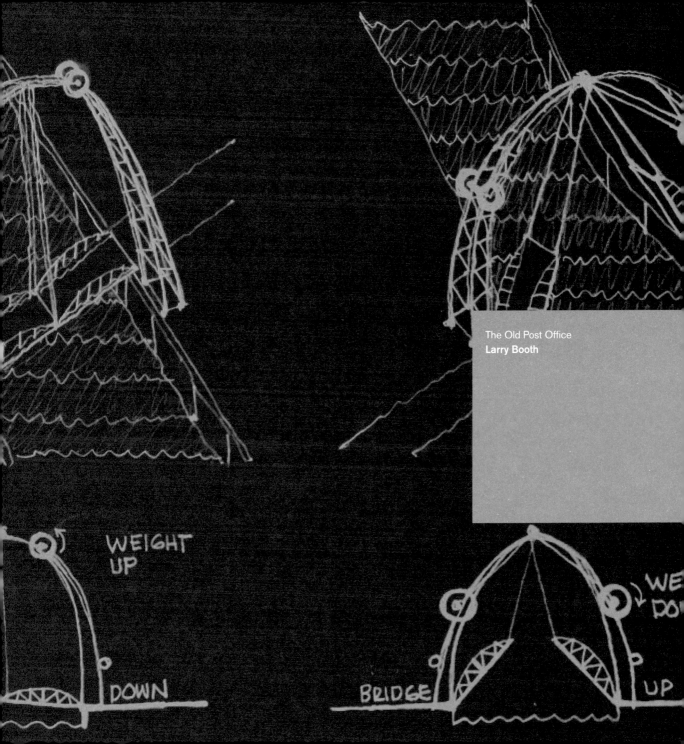

The Old Post Office
Larry Booth

WEIGHT
UP

DOWN

BRIDGE

UP

WE
DO

CHICAGO'S FIRST IN-TOWN INTERMOD[AL]

...SSWAYS DON'T MAKE LIVEABLE CITIES. KEEP HIGHWAY 290 OUT. HEAL THE
...AN AVE. AND DESPLAINES. LET THE LOOP EXTEND INTO THE UNDERUSED SOUTH...
...TING JOBS BACK TO THE CITY MEANS "SERVICE SECTOR" (80% OF US GNP) - HIGH...
...PEOPLE WHO SEEK MOBILITY, CONVENIENCE, AND LIFESTYLE. A BOLD PUBLI...
...N DEVELOPMENT WILL PROVIDE FOR 8,000 JOBS, 1700 APARTMENTS LOCA...
...E OF CHICAGO WITH TOTAL TRANSPORTATION NEEDS EFFICIENTLY PO...
...Y BELONGS WITH TRANSPORTATION.

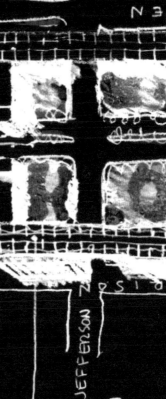

• CIRCU...
IS SI...
LANDS...
IS DIS...
CITY

• BOTH
HEAD...
UPPER...
ROOF
APA...
TOWN...
HEA...

• MID...
800,000
HEAD...
FOR
(HOF...
WAS
WHE...

DESPLAINES N/S. DESPLAINES

BUREN

JEFFERSON

DESPLAINES

CLINTON

...GRESS (HIGHWAY 290)
...RMINATES WITH

...P. LIGHT
...F DESPLAINES
...STEAD OF WELLS
...DESPLAINES FEEDER N/S.

• SBC CORPORATE
HEADQUARTERS
800,000 SF (THEY
CAN...E IN WITH

...STAYS BECAUSE
O...TRANSPORTATION
FOR EMPLOYEES)

...GRESS BECOMES
...BAN PARKWAY
...OUND LEVEL IS A
...MMUNITY INDOOR -
...RE RESTAURANTS,
...JOBS ETC - PEDESTRIAN / RCV
...RONMENT

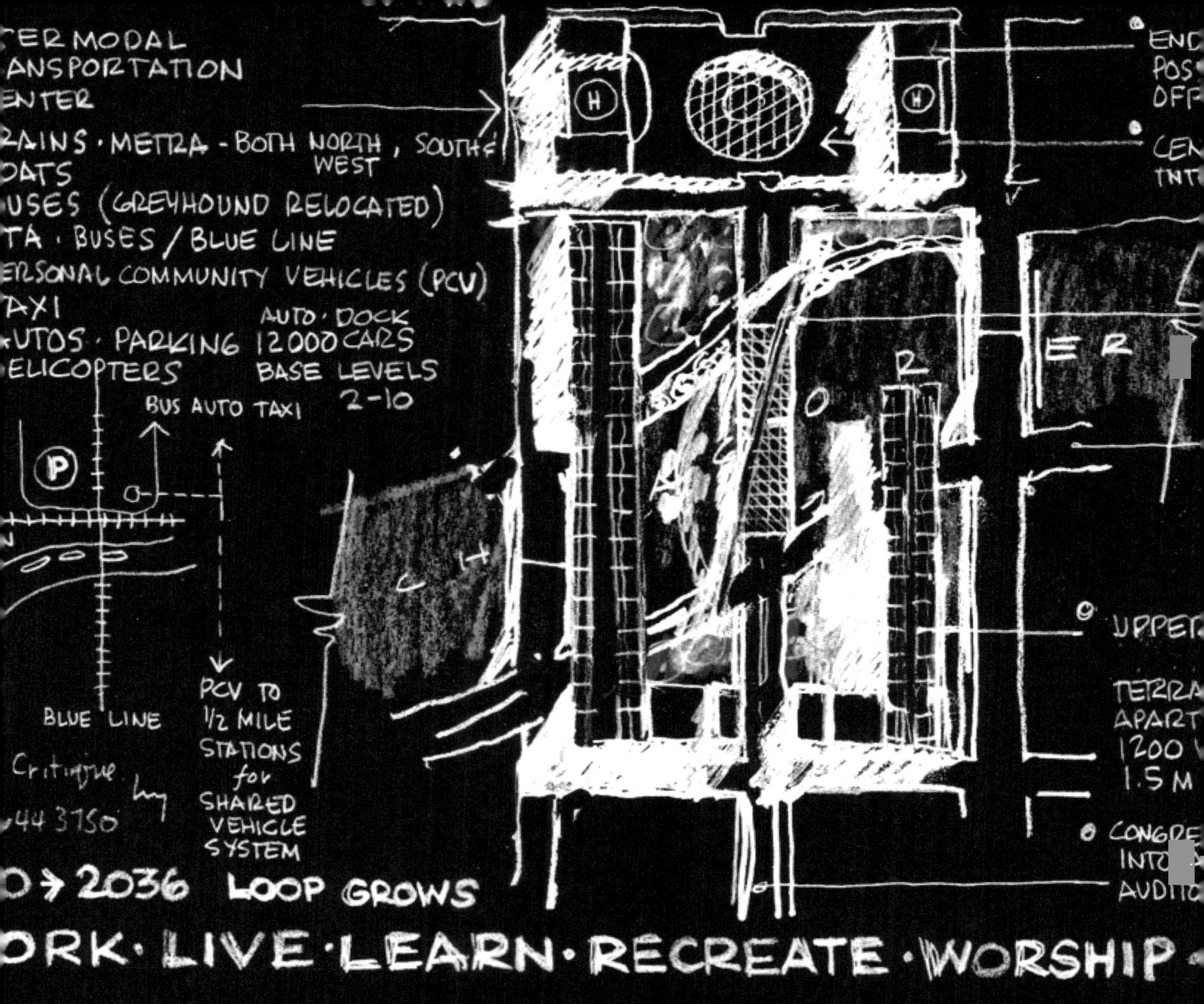

TER MODAL TRANSPORTATION CENTER

TRAINS · METRA - BOTH NORTH , SOUTH & WEST
BOATS
BUSES (GREYHOUND RELOCATED)
TA . BUSES / BLUE LINE
PERSONAL COMMUNITY VEHICLES (PCV)
TAXI
AUTOS. PARKING 12,000 CARS
HELICOPTERS
BUS AUTO TAXI

AUTO · DOCK
BASE LEVELS 2-10

BLUE LINE

PCV TO ½ MILE STATIONS for SHARED VEHICLE SYSTEM

Critique by
444 3150

→ 2036 LOOP GROWS

ORK · LIVE · LEARN · RECREATE · WORSHIP

ENG POS OFF

GEN INT

UPPER

TERRA APART 1200 1.5 M

CONGRE INTO AUDITO

155

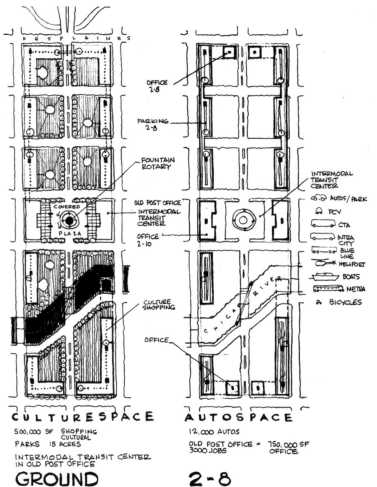

DESPLAINES

OFFICE
2-8

PARKING
2-8

FOUNTAIN
ROTARY

COVERED
CULTURAL
PLAZA

OLD POST OFFICE
INTERMODAL
TRANSIT
CENTER
OFFICE
2-10

INTERMODAL
TRANSIT
CENTER

AUTOS/PARK

PCV

CTA

INTRA
CITY

BLUE
LINE

HELIPORT

BOATS

METRA

BICYCLES

CHICAGO RIVER

CULTURE
SHOPPING

OFFICE

C U L T U R E S P A C E   A U T O S P A C E

500,000 SF SHOPPING
                CULTURAL
PARKS 15 ACRES

INTERMODAL TRANSIT CENTER
IN OLD POST OFFICE

12,000 AUTOS

OLD POST OFFICE ≈ 750,000 SF
3000 JOBS   OFFICE

GROUND   2-8

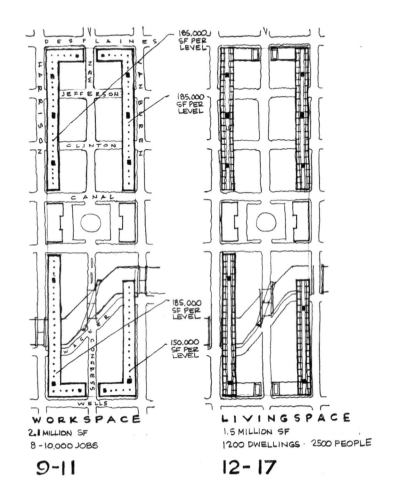

WORKSPACE
2.1 MILLION SF
8-10,000 JOBS

9-11

LIVINGSPACE
1.5 MILLION SF
1200 DWELLINGS · 2500 PEOPLE

12-17

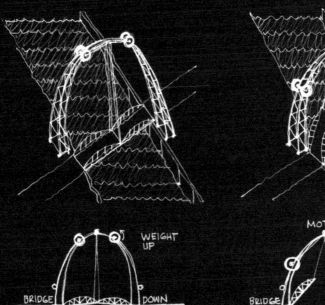

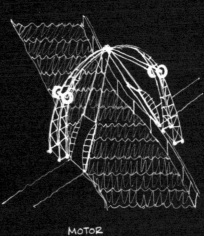

158

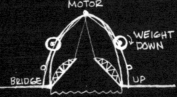

WEIGHT
UP

BRIDGE   DOWN

MOTOR

WEIGHT
DOWN

BRIDGE   UP

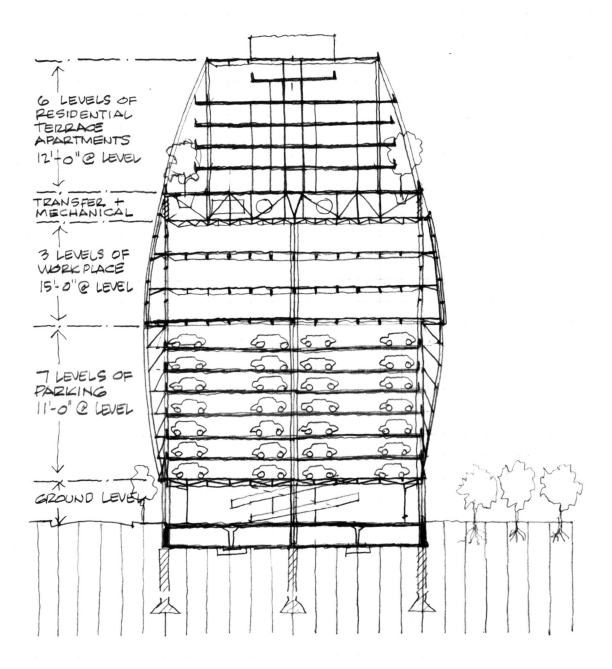

6 LEVELS OF
RESIDENTIAL
TERRACE
APARTMENTS
12'-0" @ LEVEL

TRANSFER +
MECHANICAL

3 LEVELS OF
WORK PLACE
15'-0" @ LEVEL

7 LEVELS OF
PARKING
11'-0" @ LEVEL

GROUND LEVEL

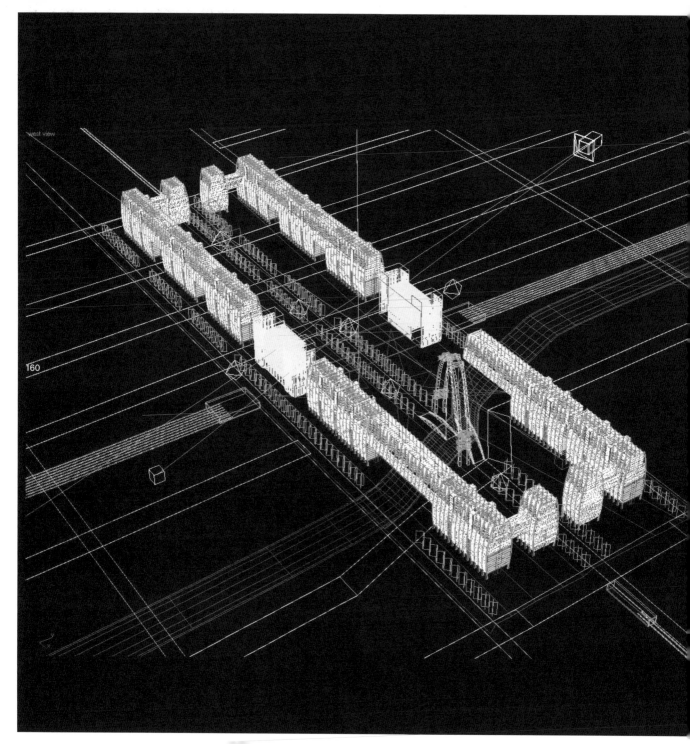

TIGERMAN
Larry, you recall, had the post office, as a sort of gateway. He did a black and white building about Chicago and its well-known racism and how things are sort of getting better or something of a gateway with linked figures.
I think it's problematic in the sense of, you know, I see these projects as visionary, but not in a jokey way.

BEEBY
I think it's kind of representative of a vision and ideas I suppose. It's a curious idea to hang a scheme on.

JOHNSON
What does it have to do with the Post Office?

TIGERMAN
I'm fond of all of you and I see it's my job to help you all and have you present your best possible work.

ROSS BARNEY
I don't think that I mind the core idea though. Congress Parkway representing the division of Chicago might be a valid investigation. I think this is a very personal idea. He's telling us what he thinks, and it happens to be the Post Office site.

LOHAN
But isn't the – by making one black and one white internalizing the division even though they link hands? I mean, what is he suggesting? How are we overcoming this? Isn't that really what should be addressed.

JAHN
The building isn't going to make a difference.

TIGERMAN
This is Larry's Post Office scheme.
And, if you remember, he had a scheme earlier that we all kind of – or some of us anyway – I certainly will take responsibility for it, didn't think a lot of. So he's come up with another scheme. It's actually pretty interesting in that he's spreading it out and not having a single focus.

JOHNSON
Where does Congress parkway go?
It's got to go underneath or something.

BEEBY
I think the idea was to actually have it end in the interchange here and not enter the loop at that point. That's my understanding of what he wanted to do.

JOHNSON
It's like you can have Kahn's scheme for Philadelphia or another series of Dirk's towers. It has to end in something.

TIGERMAN
Well, I think its a problem him not being here.

The Old Post Office
Larry Booth

Mr. Booth received his Bachelor of Arts from Stanford University in 1958. He continued his education at Harvard University and received a Bachelor of Architecture from Massachusetts Institute of Technology in 1960. He founded Booth and Nagle in 1966, beginning his professional practice.
He is NCARB certified, a Fellow of the American Institute of Architects, and is a registered architect in Illinois, Kentucky, Michigan, Minnesota, Ohio, and North Carolina.
He has been awarded numerous professional honors and has participated in several professional activities including : Reynolds Award Jury; American Academy in Rome (jury for the Rome Prize 1979 & 1984); Chicago Historical Society, Paul M. Angle Lecture 1983; various national and state AIA award juries; MIT visiting committee, Department of Architecture 1984-90; and a National Endowment for the Arts, panelist.

with
Adam Berkelhamer
Bill Joern
Brandon Perkins

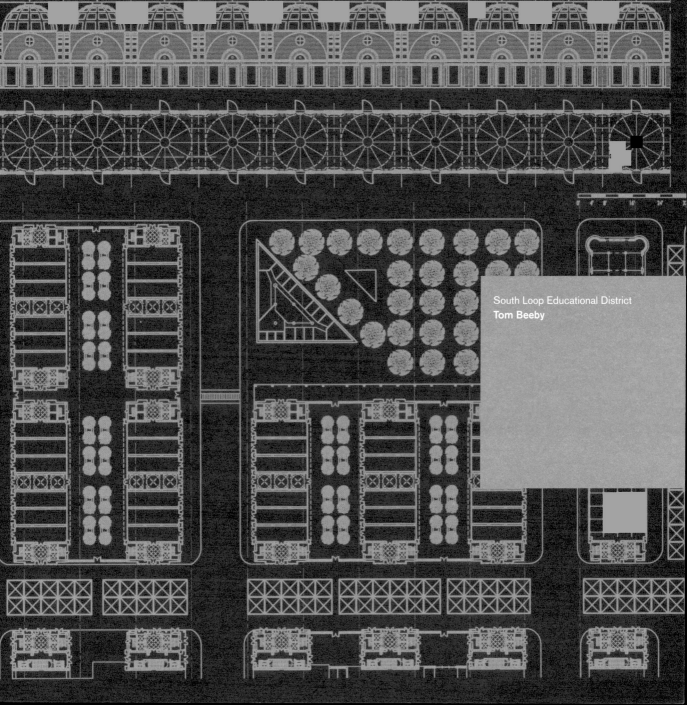

South Loop Educational District
Tom Beeby

The unplanned and unprece-dented occupation of a large portion of the Loop by over 50,000 students every working day suggests the City of Chicago could entertain new generalized strategies for the future of the central business district.

Plagued by decades of competition from North Michigan Avenue and the suburbs, the Loop is crowded with landmark buildings, underappreciated office space and new, over-built structures. The old and the new co-exist uneasily (looking either to Burnham or Hilberseimer), on blocks planned for smaller structures with bigger sites. Where older buildings may

have internal public right-of-ways and where new buildings may have ceded large or small public plazas, apparent gains in the public realm are reversible, at the discretion, not to say whim, of the private landowner.

Not-for-profit educational institutions have moved into the Loop and South Loop to take advantage of cheap available building stock accompanied by an anti-

quated but functioning central transit system which serves both neighborhoods and suburbs, an important asset for students who don't own cars. These advantages could serve other segments of society and sectors of business equally well. A major resettlement of the Loop is now possible before it becomes a truly dysfunctional central business district.

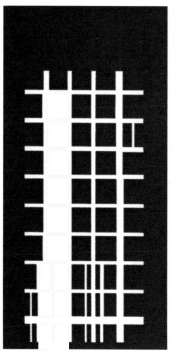

(a)

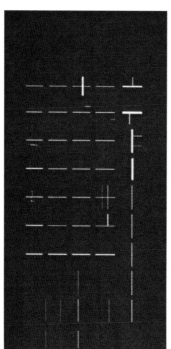

(b)

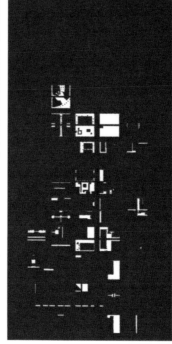

(c)

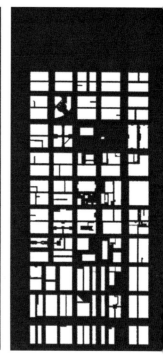

(d)

(left)

Analysis of public/private realm in Loop area

(a) The Street Pattern

(b) The Alley Pattern

(c) Publicly Accessible Space in the Private Realm

(d) Built vs. Open Space Today

(below)

Analysis of solid/void in Loop Area

(e) In the Green Tube Passengers

(f) Experience Park Landscape

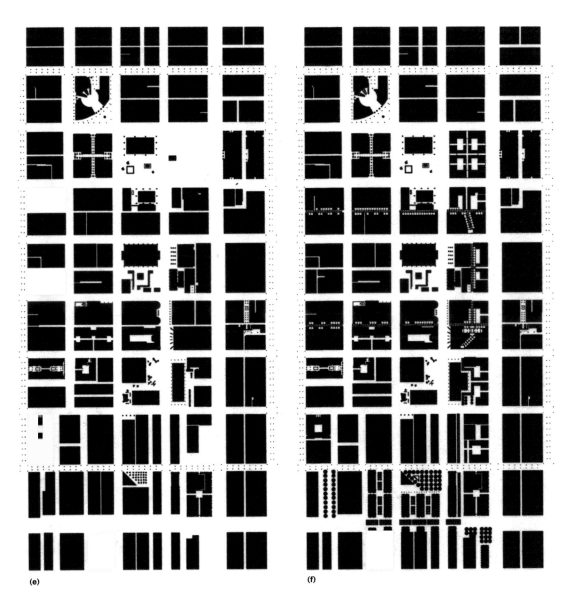

(e)

(f)

1 Convert underutilized office and loft buildings with adequate light and air into a mix of subsidized and market rate housing. Convert buildings not appropriate for housing into office/studio incubator space to encourage small, owner-operated start-ups.

2 Construct new mid-rise buildings with combined market rate and subsidized housing accompanied by necessary amenities on site. Arrange these new buildings around quarter block courtyards and limit cornice heights to 150' to guarantee adequate air and light in perpetuity. Use bay sizes, floor-to-floor heights and fenestration consistent with the idea of convertibility between residential, commercial and institutional uses. Provide office/studio space adjacent to each residence. Include site amenities such as planned landscape areas, social support organizations and community facilities.

3 Construct continuous east/west enclosed public arcades in the right-of-way of both Calhoun Place and Marble Place. Spur redevelopment of small owner-operated shops internal to the block without disturbing external street retail patterns. Claim the right of eminent domain to re-establish public access at mid-block inside existing properties built on vacated alleys.

4 Expand the pedestrian experience with organic farmers' markets selling locally grown produce and providing an alternate food source.

5 Provide owner operated food concessions in common courtyards at ground level, offering a variety of lunch and dinner foods as an alternative for busy city-dwellers who may not have the time or inclination to cook at home.

6 Build facilities for truly continuing education on the top levels of new buildings to include child and elder care, elementary, secondary and vocational schools as well as retraining centers for immigrants, the working poor and the unemployed. Accommodate gymnasia and auditoria on the upper floors.

7 Create secure public gardens, both at ground level and on rooftops, to introduce the soothing power of nature into a dense urban situation.

8 Construct necessary but limited parking and delivery access below grade only.

9 Eliminate below grade pedways & upper-level concourses concentrating the pedestrian experience in the right-of-way of certain streets.

10 Encourage diverse architectural expressions appropriate to a democratic society while searching for the common themes of quality which have always raised Chicago architecture above the ordinary.

(below)

Historical Forms of Expression for frame
Construction in Chicago

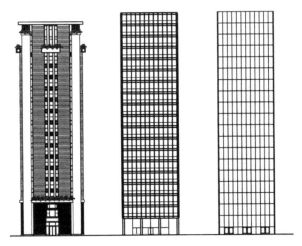

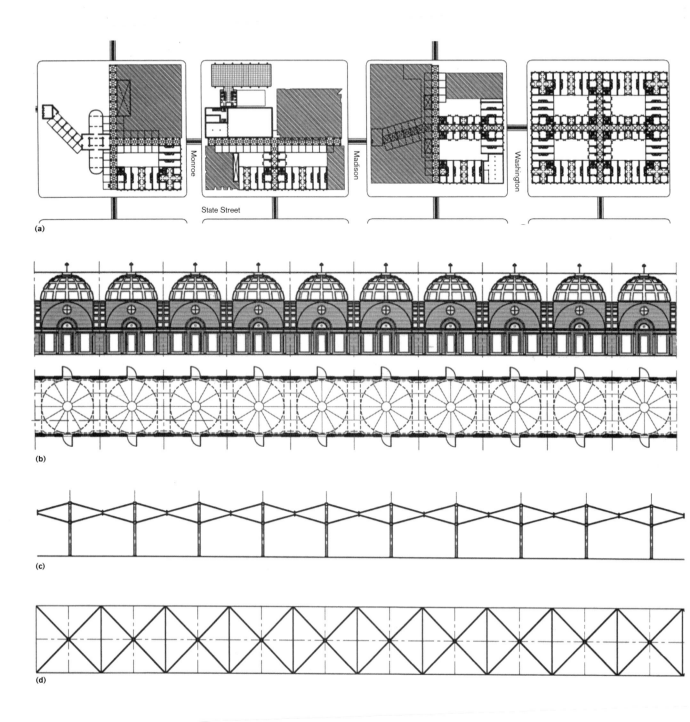

Monroe

State Street

Madison

Washington

(a)

(b)

(c)

(d)

(left)
a) Partial Loop Resettlement Plan
b) Arcade Plan
c) Market Elevation
d) Market Plan

(right)
e) Retail and Business
   Floor Plans
f) Artisan and Institutional
   Floor Plans

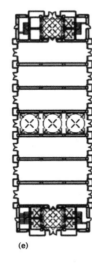
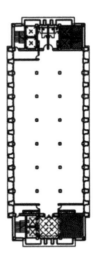

(e)

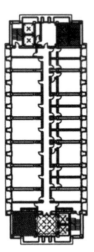
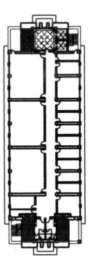

(f)

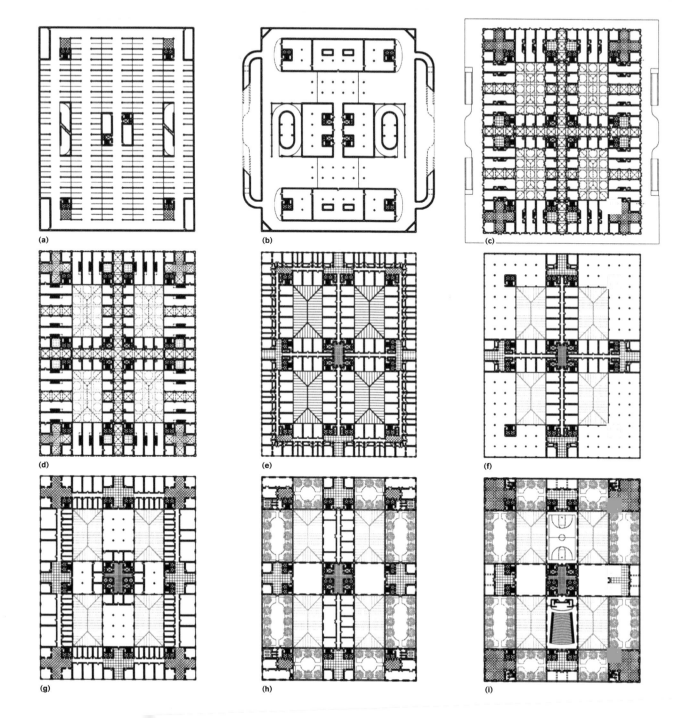

(a) (b) (c)

(d) (e) (f)

(g) (h) (i)

(left)

Plans for full block resettlement

a) Parking
b) Loading
c) Retail
d) Residential/Office
e) Housing

(f) Mechanical/Administrative
(g) Class Rooms/Offices
(h) Community Houses/Services
(i) Central Assembly/Community Meeting

(below)

Elevations for full block resettlement

(j)   North/South Elevations
(k) East/West Elevations
(l)   Transverse Section
(m) Longitudinal Section

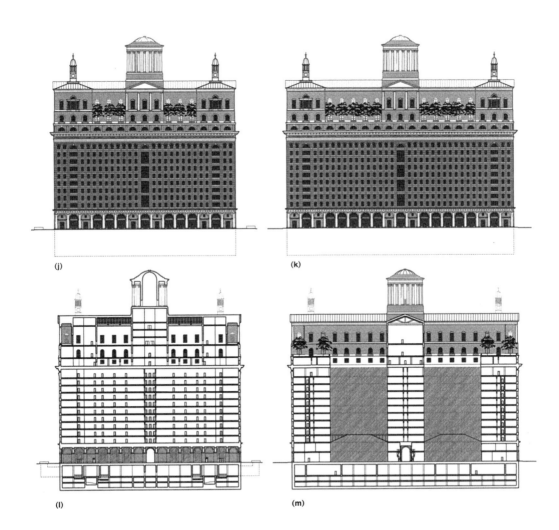

(j)

(k)

(l)

(m)

BEEBY

I have the students in the Loop.

I'm familiar with situations where cities don't like universities to move in like this because it means they're losing tax base because of the non-profit. So people like New Haven and Evanston are fighting to keep the university from building things.

So I got to thinking that maybe this is not such a great thing, but then, on the other hand, the students actually bring life to the city.

Then I had this notion that maybe we should think how the Loop is laid out and how it works. I tried to work out a type of development that would give you smaller increments of development and allow the blocks to be built in a kind of readable way. So we focus on State and Congress the two places it made the most sense.

The idea was to add in a secondary system in the city that would move down toward the alleys and make them arcades. Build little vaulted structure which then have doors on them into the backs of these buildings - you're setting up a secondary retail roof in the city that's under cover.

TIGERMAN
So this is a secret part of Chicago.

Yeah. This is a subversive system.

Well, that assumes that there was a blockage. So you're blocking – one building type was going to block the other people out.

172

SMITH
Well, it's sort of like – isn't it sort of like European facades?

Yeah, exactly.

SMITH
That's very appropriate for Chicago because we have all this pedestrian movement. And you're always outside. This would be great.

Yeah. It's actually aligned with where everybody walks down Washington and Adams. I'm trying to figure out a way to heat them.

SMITH
You could use the air from the subways, the air is the subways is always 50 to 60 degrees.

BARNEY
You can imagine this alley being filled in and the knitting together of it is very intimate.

TIGERMAN
Your timing is impeccable. You've traditionalized the city.

Not really. It's not really traditionalized.

TIGERMAN
I'm being cute.
Can I tell you what's interesting about it, too. The Loop on the second floor has all these people that can't afford to pay big rents.

They're getting kicked out.

TIGERMAN
But these are places for them.

South Loop
Educational District
Tom Beeby

Mr. Beeby is Professor (Adjunct) of Architectural Design at Yale University School of Architecture. He was dean of the school from 1985 to 1991, and director of the School of Architecture at the University of Illinois at Chicago from 1979 to 1985. As Principal in Charge of Design with his firm, Hammond Beeby Rupert Ainge Inc., he has overseen the planning and design of a variety of projects including Chicago's Harold Washington Library Center, The Hole In The Wall Gang Camp in Connecticut and the more recent Baker Institute at Rice University. A recently completed project under his direction is the Music and Dance Theater Chicago located in Millennium Park on Michigan Avenue. He has written and lectured on the work of Louis Sullivan, Frank Lloyd Wright, Mies van der Rohe and the relationship of ornament to structure, including the article *The Grammar of Ornament/ Ornament as Grammar* published in *Via*, volume 3, in 1977. Mr. Beeby received his B. Arch. from Cornell University and his M. Arch. from Yale University.

Afterward

Lee Bey

Take a look around Chicago. Skyscrapers and cranes compete for space along the skyline. Earthmovers and backhoes are just as stuck in traffic these days as cars and buses.

Things are getting built here. And while that seems like a given in Chicago – the city that works, and all that – it was not that long ago when not even the air moved. Things were so stagnant in the 1970s and 1980s, even a misstep such as turning State Street into a pedestrian mall was seen as progress in 1979 because, heck, at least it was something. The early 1990s were the watched pot that would take six years to boil.

Now Chicago can fashion a world-class urban park out of the thin air over the Illinois Central tracks east of Michigan Avenue downtown; it can re-bend sections of Lake Shore Drive like pipe cleaners and it can turn a seedy run of stores into a new city college –

which is what's happening now at 63rd and Halsted. The city is taking down its monstrous high-rise ghettoes and is replacing them (cross your fingers here) with viable and socially sustainable new communities.

It's Chicago becoming *Chicago* again; building, reworking and reshaping this 225 square mile lakeside canvas. Each draft is better than the one before it.

It is miraculous, yes. But how much of it is truly visionary? This is not at all a swipe at what has been accomplished. However, we can't lose sight of the fact that Chicago architecture and design, at its best, is not just good-looking and popular, but visionary. This is the context for this book of great ideas that you are now holding. And it comes at a critical time for Chicago. Yes, we have tamed some unruly corners of the Loop and brought salvation to countless down-and-out blocks.

The picture looks fine, but step back a few paces. There is a larger work to be done; a higher order to be maintained.

The projects represented in this book underscore that fact. There are design ideas here that point to new horizons. There are notions and paradigms that are fresh and just a bit heady. There is also a subtle but insistent message between these two covers: Architecture and urban planning in current (and future) Chicago has to do more than appeal to the eye of the aesthete. Buildings have to do more than look good. Urban design needs a higher goal than simply creating a proper box to introduce buildings, trees, roads, berms and visually appropriate street furniture.

What we build – particularly if it's a significant project – must have a hand in changing lives and creating opportunity for Chicago residents.

173

This book is also a reminder that architecture and urban design must have a larger hand in fostering new economies and bolstering old ones.

Pie-in-the-sky? Good. So was reversing the natural flow of the Chicago River. Preserving the lakefront for recreational use, creating the world's tallest building, the world's busiest airport, the 1893 Columbian Exposition and a host of other things were also pretty unlikely. Yet they all happened.

You will find a mechanical parking tower proposed for Chinatown. This is the kind of vision – the spark of genius – that is a part of Chicago's best stuff. Drop off your car and the robotic insides of this tower will take your car and store it inside. Each of the 4200 cars parked around circular bays could be retrieved mechanically – dispensed upon payment as easily as getting a can of soda from a vending machine.

It's a cool way to park a car. But it will also give crowded,

compact Chinatown something it needs to better connect it to McCormick Place and Downtown: parking. The tall tower marks Chinatown, a neighborhood that is so cut off by the expressway and rail lines that "you'd zoom by it and never know you passed it," said Dirk Lohan, architect of the parking tower.

With the proposal, an outpost becomes a crossroads. There must be a dozen places in the city where this concept, link to rail, would work such as the areas around Midway airport or even the city's Metra rail stations.

The best of Chicago's architecture and urban planning is visionary. Mies van der Rohe's 860-880 Lake Shore Drive; the Columbian Exposition; the vast boulevard system; the skyscraper; the preservation of the lakefront– the list goes on – were all lessons in how the built environment could make living better, easier, uplifting or more profitable. They were

also benchmarks in design and engineering. They solve real problems and break ground.

The work in this book demands to be judged that way. It commands an evaluation at a depth and rigor greater than simple praise-or-pan judgments of individual buildings and schemes. An aside: can we please – please! – dispense with the quarterly hand ringing over whether Chicago has lost its architectural edge, nerve, groove, will, heart or what-have-you? Four years ago, the tastemakers said we were on a downward slide architecturally. Then, overnight, the winds shifted and we've apparently regained what we've lost, thanks to Millennium Park and a handful of good-looking new residential towers.

If that's all it took, were we really so bad off after all? And if we were that bad off, architecturally, would Millennium Park and Skybridge be enough to save us? Best to leave the superficial "hot or not" assess

ments to celebrity watchers and nightclub door men. Architectural design and urba planning – and this book und scores this – requires a more nuanced and deliberate look.

The book presents a plan to build greenhouses and gardens along the branches of the Chicago River.

"The Ohio feeder ramp (the long ramp that connects the Kennedy Expressway to dow town) is a true feeder ramp now," mused Jeanne Gang, the architect who authored the plan. Is this a folly? Don't dismiss this proposal so easi The plan is a thoughtful nudg the city should consider as it advances its "green" ethos fro the current realm of flowerboxe and median planters. Given th number of restaurants and homes in this region that are in need of fruits and vegetabl on an daily, if not hourly basis this idea boils down to one chi benefit: jobs – plain and simp There are quality-of-life ramific tions as well. The spaces alon the river would be lush, visually interesting points, a respite from the bustle of the city.

It also shows what ought to be the next level of architecture and urban design in this town.

Visionary architecture also anticipates the future. This is admittedly tricky ground. Think of all the renderings of visions past: soulless skyscrapers sitting in a spaghetti bowl of limited access high speed roadways. Stark buildings on concrete plazas. Glassy, tube-like (although Habitrail-like might be a better description) overhead walkways.

If these proposals seem laughable now, it's partly because they didn't actually solve a real problem. This was set design, not urban design. But in this book, there are more realistic takes on the future. They are visionary because the architects have taken an issue that is small today and they have tracked it – like actuaries – to a point in the future where a solution will be needed.

Cemetery space is shrinking around the region and in developed countries across the globe. The funeral industry shouldn't solve this problem alone. One proposal in this book sees an architectural way to tackle this issue: to turn the old Main Post Office into a municipal mausoleum.

This massive building straddling the mouth of the Eisenhower Expressway would have halls, chapels, a rooftop memorial, and niches for remains. The building would be refitted inside and out to create a respectful place to honor thousands.

"Very soon, we have to rethink how we want Chicagoans remembered," said John Ronan, architect of the proposal.

This is simply an ingenious proposal. The plan provides a new use for a building that – let's face it – is awfully tough to reuse because of its size, condition and over-the-express-way configuration. It solves a real problem and creates a template that might be able to be applied throughout the city.

How many neo-classical bank buildings around the country are sitting empty, playing for time, until either time, weather or a drugstore chain demolished them? Maybe this is a way to reuse them.

And intended or not, the proposal is a subtle nod to the growing dissatisfaction with the typical funeral-then-follow-the-black-limousines-to-the-cemetery ritual. The municipal mausoleum plan foresees funeral barges traveling down the Chicago River to this magnificent edifice.

The other plans are equal but why give away every plot twist here? Dig in and read. You'll find these visions are not a wake-up call for Chicago architecture, but a mark that must be hit – and that's a great deal more valuable.

 As we rebuild this great city, our work must be imbued with the desire to create a higher and better order along the way. This book tells us so. We'd do well to listen, learn, and then *build*.

First and foremost, the Editors wish to thank all fourteen architects who participated in this event: Carol Ross Barney, Thomas Beeby, Laurence Booth, Jeanne Gang, Douglas Garofalo, Helmut Jahn, Ralph Johnson, Ronald Krueck, Dirk Lohan, Bradley Lynch, John Ronan, Adrian Smith, Joseph Valerio and David Woodhouse. Without hesitation, they committed their time and extraordinary talents to this project. Throughout the year-long process they produced copious amounts of work even as they remained vigilant to our collective vision for this book. We also wish to thank Lee Bey, Robert Bruegmann and James DeStefano for their unique perspectives on this enterprise.

Even though those listed above worked pro bono, financial and promotional support was necessarily required to successfully bring these concepts to a publishable state. The Chicago Central Area Committee (CCAC), a civic organization dedicated to the improvement of Chicago's downtown, was instrumental in providing monetary support as well as establishing venues for presenting (and discussing) the visionary concepts herein.

Special recognition is due to those within the CCAC who early on recognized the importance of a document such as this: Carrie Hightman, president of the CCAC, for her leadership in seeing this project to completion; Thomas Klutznick for his timely financial support; Richard Solomon and The Graham Foundation for Advanced Studies in the Fine Arts for their generous grant; Julian D'Esposito of Mayer, Brown, Rowe and Maw, along with Virginia Aronson of Sidney Austin Brown & Wood for providing hours of court transcriptions necessary to document the process; John McCarter, President of the Field Museum of Chicago, for offering to host the initial public presentation; and Richard Hanson, Principal of Mesa Development Corporation, for his offering virtually the entire 2005 Urban Land Institute's lecture agenda for seven presentations featuring each pair of architects.

Our thanks to Alisa Wolfson for her unique book design, to Craig Skorborg, who provided his photographic services without compensation, and to Tasha Olivo, the court reporter who suffered through innumerable hours of architect's mumblings.

Thank you all for your commitment to this book and to this glorious City.

Stanley Tigerman and
William Martin

Designed:
A. Wolfson Design, Co.
Published:
Chicago Central Area Committee
Printed:
Rider Dickerson, Chicago
Architectural Drawings provided by individual Architects.
Copyright ©2005